EASTWARD TO THE SUN

EASTWARD
TO THE SUN

By
Sanford Calvin Yoder

HERALD PRESS
SCOTTDALE, PENNSYLVANIA

TO EMMA

My loving wife and companion, who by her sacrifice and helpfulness made possible my labors in the Lord

PREFACE

Early in my childhood I somehow received the impression that the sun has its home in the east and that it started from there each day on its long tour through the sky. Just how it returned to its quarters for the night never occurred to me nor can I recall the incident that led to this conception of the celestial traveler that has brought light and warmth to the earth since the fourth day of the creation week.

I had always planned in my childish simplicity to go someday and explore the place of the "tabernacle for the sun" from which it goes forth each day "as a bridegroom coming out of his chamber, and rejoiceth as a strong man to run a race." Though this early vision has long since been dispelled, the desire to see this fabled land with its multitude of people and its marvels and wonders has always remained with me.

The opportunity to satisfy my curiosity, however, did not come until after I had retired from my position on the Mennonite Board of Missions and Charities through whose activities I was brought into contact with the affairs of the lands and people that were embraced in the journey which is described in this volume. When I was first approached with the proposition of making the trip, I questioned the value of such an undertaking and the worth of any contribution I could make to the cause I was to represent. There were also matters of distance, travel inconveniences and any and all other problems that one would encounter along the way. These things loomed large in the distance, but when approached their importance and seriousness diminished. What forebodings I had of a tedious trip disappeared and the journey though arduous and tiring turned out to be pleasant and enjoyable.

When it was suggested that some of my experiences, observations, and meditations should be compiled and set up in some permanent form I took up the task with many misgivings. I know full well what people say about writers who spend brief periods in new lands, among strange people, and then return to their homes and "write a book." It is a precarious undertaking. The quibs and jibes of those who criticize such ventures are well founded. This is especially true when the task is in the hands of novices who pose as experts on the social, economic, religious, and political problems of the countries they visit and include "quack" or hastily formed prescriptions and panaceas for all the ills they have seen.

There is, however, a type of material that is often better represented by the casual visitor than by the more mature observer. Long acquaintance and association with people of widely different manners and ways of life tends to dampen the lustre of the newness and strangeness that is at first so appealing and reduces it to the commonplace where it loses its interest. Hence it is not my purpose to even pretend to be a historian, an economist, a political scientist, or a dispenser of counsel or cures for the ailments of the lands I visited. I am simply a traveler who has followed the roads across the world and have jotted down such of my experiences, observations, bits of history, and "what-not" as have caught my fancy, engaged my interest, or stirred my curiosity as I mingled with the people in their villages, cities, and towns or met them in their homes, or along the highway and streets.

The journey began in July, 1949, and took me through parts of England, Belgium, Luxembourg, France, Switzerland, Germany, Holland, and Italy during my two months' stay in Europe. In nearly all of these countries the Mennonite Central Committee had its centers and personnel through which relief work was carried on during and after the war. These places became home to me and the relief workers were my counselors and guides and made my stay pleasant and worth while.

My final destination and the high point of my trip was India. Words fail to express my emotions when I stepped ashore at Bombay. It was winter time—snowless and warm. The temperature would have almost justified the conclusion that the sun had its home close by. Day by day this land of enchantment—its landscape, its people, customs, tradition and life—unfolded before my eyes. I saw the colorful throngs in the cities and villages, along the jungle roads and at the wayside bazaars. I also saw the churches, the missionaries and their homes, and above all the fruit of their labors—the Indian Christians.

Two months was too brief a time to enable one to see all there is to be seen and to do all one would like to do. India is large, complex, and beautiful. A westerner becomes almost overwhelmed with the complicated intricacies of its customs, traditions, and the details of its life. But it has furnished me with a world of interesting material with which to fill memory's storehouse, and as the years come and go I shall draw heavily upon it for inspiration as I see again in fancy this lovely race in its romantic land.

SANFORD CALVIN YODER

Goshen, Indiana
1952

CONTENTS

I. *Travel Preparations* _____ 1

II. *From New York to London* _____ 5

III. *In and Out of London Town* _____ 11

IV. *Across Flander's Fields and Luxembourg* ___ 24

V. *The Alsatian Land and Lorraine* _____ 33

VI. *Charming Switzerland* _____ 41

VII. *Sunny Italy* _____ 53

VIII. *Trailways Through Germany* _____ 68

IX. *Along the Dikes and Canals of Holland* ___ 81

X. *Where the Ghosts Walk* _____ 91

XI. *From Venice to Bombay* _____ 104

XII. *Hail India!* _____ 116

XIII. *India's People* _____ 128

XIV. *India's Villages and Ways of Life* _____ 139

XV. *The Mennonite Church in India* _____ 150

XVI. *From Station to Station* _____ 158

XVII. *The Institutions of the Church in India* ___ 172

XVIII. *India, What of the Night!* _____ 184

XIX. *Glimpses Along India's Highways* _____ 199

XX. *Sailing with the Strathmore* _____ 208

ILLUSTRATIONS

OPPOSITE PAGE 20

A village in rural England
Westminster Abbey, London
A Royal procession from Buckingham Palace
Gutting Herring in England
Stoke Poges Church, England
Bullange, Belgium
A typical peasant farm home, Luxembourg
Procession of the Penitentes, Belgium
Interior of a peasant home, Luxembourg

OPPOSITE PAGE 84

A Netherlands country scene
Church where Menno Simons preached, Holland
Monument to Menno Simons, Holland
A German village
Vineyards on the hillsides in the Palatinate
The author beside Menno Simons monument, Germany
Churches dot the landscape in Alsatian land
Swiss children. Jungfrau in the background
Grape harvest in Switzerland
The Grossmunster Church in Switzerland

OPPOSITE PAGE 132

Naples, with Mt. Vesuvius in the background
A gate in the old Roman wall, Rome, Italy
Entrance to the Suez Canal
Ford agency at Aden
In the hills of North India
The Taj Mahal, Agra, India
Kailasa Temple, Ellora, India
Dr. Jonathan Yoder after the tiger hunt
The post office, Calcutta, India
Gardens of the government house, India

I

TRAVEL PREPARATIONS

India, fabled land of religion and romance! Who that has ever heard of it has not longed to see it? For years, while serving as an official of a board of missions that operated in that country, it was my desire to visit the land and its people. But now that this dream of other years was about to become a reality my spirit faltered. The connections that once stimulated my desire to travel thither were severed when my thirty-two years of service came to an end. Most of the missionaries now serving under the board I was to represent had received their appointment during the time I was in the office of secretary or president. Those ties were precious to me but since others now occupied the positions that once were mine, I felt deeply that there was no longer any need for my going and that someone should make the trip whose connections with the organization could bring into its counsels the knowledge and experience gained from a personal visit such as this one was to be.

Besides the foregoing objections there was also the possibility that a long journey, such as this, might become strenuous and difficult. Then, too, there were the attachments of home and family which grow with the years, and one hesitates to separate himself from them for long periods of time, especially when great distances are involved. The trees and shrubs around the place whose nurture and care I had in hand from the time they were transplanted called for my attention. When I last stroked the silvery bark of the birch trees, the green leaves of the elms and maples, the spikes of the evergreens, they all voiced, it seemed, a protest against my going. Then there was the mole, ungracious and unimaginative little creature, that persisted in uprooting my lawn and garden—my wife's garden—and caused me no little concern. The ugly little mounds and brown streaks across the velvety sward showed clearly the course of his operations. Thus far he had survived every design upon his life—poison, drowning, and whatever devices the combined wisdom of the community had to offer—and had carried on successfully his underground depredations.

But more serious than objections of lawn and trees and shrubs, was the illness of my ninety-one-year-old mother. One night a few days before the ship was to sail the telephone rang near the hour of midnight. The voice that followed the wire from across the wide spaces of the West informed us that she had gone home. Several days later while I was en route to the city by the sea, the port of embarkation, she was laid away in the little wind-swept cemetery on the Great Plains that had afforded her a home the last forty years of her life.

When once one's decision is made to undertake a trip abroad or here and there around the world, a maze of details rise which have to be taken into account. First of all the examining physician insisted upon a battery of tests to determine whether I was a fit subject to journey hither and yon across the globe. The first of the series had to do with the head and chest. After a few days I was assured by the Roentologist that everything was in order in the "upstairs and attic." At later intervals the process was repeated until the ordeal was over and I was told that there was no physical unsoundness in me and was pronounced a suitable person to travel in every land and clime by land or sea or air.

Next in order came the inoculations—smallpox, tetanus, typhoid, paratyphoid, typhus, diphtheria, scarlet fever, and so on. After each one of these dermal punctures I was assured that the worst was over only to come out of the next one as groggy as ever.

But even before all the preceding preliminaries were over, proceedings for a passport had to be instituted. Once a person has established his status by convincing the authorities of State that he was born and did not come into existence in some other unorthodox way, the document may be secured with a minimum of

2

difficulty. A remission of the proper fee, accompanied by a formal application, certified by competent witnesses of identification and the number and date of previous passports, is sufficient. It is to be expected that in these times of political unrest and disturbance, all governments should be cautious about the kind of people that come and go across the frontiers of their domains. One should not be surprised or annoyed because of rigid border regulations, inspections, customs, and duties as he goes from country to country.

A journey that takes one through different climatic zones or through lands where seasonal changes are great, calls for judgment as to the provisions that should be made in the way of wearing apparel and other equipment. Seasoned tourists as a rule "travel light." They say that the traveling maturity of a person may be fairly well judged by the amount of luggage he carries with him. Hence after having journeyed across the length and breadth of our own continent, and almost the length of Latin American lands—across their pampas, into the heat of the interior, through the frigid passes of their mountains—with only two suitcases, one large and one small, I have become a stanch advocate of the doctrine of keeping one's luggage at a minimum.

After a few days in New York, getting final things in order for sailing, I left my airy and spacious room at the Governor Clinton for the pier where the *S.S. Washington* was docked. Here my credentials were checked and within a short time I was on board in a comfortable cabin which was shared by three others who were to be my roommates as far as England.

A departing ship usually presents the problem of bedlam. Relatives and friends of passengers crowd the decks until there is barely room for those who will make this their home for the duration of the voyage. After the visitors were cleared off the ship and were put ashore, they lined the railings along the dock, and stood in a "boiling sun" until their faces were dripping and their bodies raw, waving and gesturing till the whistle blew and the pilot pulled the large liner away from its mooring and set it on its way to the sea. Then with its proud nose up and its heels dug deeply into the waters, the good ship glided by the Statue of Liberty and the old Immigration Building into the broad Atlantic.

Somehow this cutting loose from the shores of one's homeland affects me strangely! When the anchors are lifted, and the last cords that tie the vessel to the shore are loosed and one sees the sky line fading, then memories of home and family and friends loom large. Happy at such a time is he who knows the security that lies in the Great Unseen Pilot who is the same by land or sea, who rules the wind and weather and has power to guide one safely to his destination.

II

FROM NEW YORK
TO LONDON

They that go down to the sea in ships,
That do business in great waters,
These see the works of the Lord;
And his wonders in the deep.
                    —Psalm 107:23, 24

Having taken an inventory of my surroundings on board ship, I found that one of my cabin mates was an Irishman, a retired official from New York City who was going back to the hills of Killarney to spend the rest of his days among his relatives. Another was a Spanish businessman who was returning to his native country for a visit and to extol the opportunities for success in the land of his adoption. The third was a German Jew, a refugee who sacrificed his fortune to get out of Germany in Hitler's day shortly before the fires of Buchenwald began to burn. Early during the Nazi rule he sensed what was coming and in one way or another succeeded in getting enough money out of the country so that he and his wife can now live comfortably the rest of their days. His return to Europe was for the purpose of salvaging what he could of his multimillion dollar mercantile business which extended through Northern Germany and into Poland.

The passenger group was what one usually finds on shipboard. Tourists and businessmen predominated. Mass was conducted every morning. Protestant worship was held on Sunday forenoon with a sizable congregation present. The latter was a strictly prayer book service conducted by a Presbyterian minister under the direction of the Captain of the ship. Shuffleboard and deck games

5

2

of various kinds were provided and were constantly in use. The swimming pool, as usual, was the most occupied portion of the ship.

The first meal of the voyage is always an event. This being a United States vessel the food was what one could get at a first-class American restaurant. The table company was pleasant and the service par excellent. Among the unusual items that appeared on the menu was "Pennsylvania Dutch Soup," which could hardly be described as "soup" and a person belonging to that clan would dubiously accept it as being "Pennsylvania Dutch." It would certainly have been disowned by any Pennsylvania Dutch housewife that I have ever learned to know.

Scenery along the North Atlantic Sea lanes is very drab and is limited to whatever the sea and sky provide. There are no island studded waters. If there were whales, sea monsters, porpoises or other species of marine life they all kept themselves securely under cover while our vessel passed by. Good weather made possible pleasant hours on deck with the newly found friends from many parts of the world. There were lovely sunsets, beautifully clouded skies, and occasionally a "pouring" rain that drove the lounging crowds under cover of decks or awnings.

Early one morning the passengers saw land—Ireland. The rolling hills looked like a beautiful checkerboard with their alternating patches of green pasture land and fields of yellow grain. Villages and farmsteads, set amid clusters of trees, adorned the landscape and made one wish to spend days among the scenes that appeared so tranquil and restful. Queenstown—Cobh as the Irish call it—is a sprawling city on the west coast of the island. In the absence of docks, lighters came alongside the ship to take off its cargo. Smart little steamers were soon loaded with the happy children of Erin or their descendants, stalwart sons and fair-haired lassies—some red—who were returning for a few weeks of rest and leisure to the country of their dreams and song, "Where the River Shannon Flows" and "Where the Wild Irish Roses Bloom." What a lovely place these people have come to and what happy folks

6

they are! Nature had done her best to prepare their ancestral home to receive its guests. Copious showers during the night left this "emerald of the sea" glistening in the morning sun, fresh and clean after its nightly bath. Great banks of clouds that looked like carded wool rose out of the sea and hung along the horizon or drifted across the sky filling the landscape with lights and shadows. One wonders what the world would be without the Irish. Where would the cities of our western countries and other lands get their policemen and how drab would be the wit and humor that stirs and cheers one's spirit were it not seasoned with Erin's brogue!

But now comes along one of the flock of inquisitors and statistic gatherers who have descended upon the earth like a plague. As usual, he comes up with a sour note which in this case threatens to ruin my vision of this enchanting land by laying before me the bare facts of what is happening to its delightful folk. He maintains that within the last one hundred years, 1840-1940, the population of that part now known as the Irish Republic has fallen from six and one half million to a fraction less than three million. According to his findings it is no longer a land of beautiful colleens and romantic lovers. Sixty-five per cent of its people, he asserted, are unmarried, seven per cent are widows. Only twenty-eight per cent are married. Since his compilations take no account of widowers it is reasonable to assume that there are none—their wives outlived them all! Only two out of five between the ages of 30 to 35 have risked matrimony. The lads and lassies of the "Old Sod" must cease to dodge Don Cupid, he insists, or its population will become as extinct as dodo birds. At this rate of decline, he assures us, there will soon be no one left but bachelors and old maids and when the race finally dies out who will bury the last one? Since there will not be anyone to start contrition proceedings, his future will be hopeless.

This outlook left me cold, completely deflated, flat and hopeless as a punctured tire. What a drab, uninspiring prospect these happy, enthusiastic young Irish who sailed with us, came to! I

7

shall always be thankful for the notes I had entered in my journal before this statistician came up, for otherwise there would be nothing to write. This "Emerald Isle" according to this prophet of doom has no future and might as well be sunk to the bottom of the sea. And when his prognostications shall come to pass, the world will be a "sorry" place to contemplate. Lawlessness will likely sweep unrestrained over every land because there will be no competent policemen to maintain order. Maybe that's what's wrong now—not enough Irish on the police force!

The next morning the coast of Normandy came into view and by midafternoon we entered the rubble-filled harbor of La Havre. After much skillful maneuvering the pilots finally guided the large liner to the docks of the United States Lines. Ghosts of the carnage and destruction of the late war stalked everywhere. Fragments of vessels littered the harbor. Piles of ruins lined the waterfront and the jagged remnants of buildings partly destroyed stood like broken bodies without a soul. Barges, loaded to the limit with rubble and remains of the wreckage, pushed their desolate cargoes seaward to make way for new structures that were beginning to rear their heads above their gruesome surroundings. All these tokens reminded us of the fierceness with which the battle raged when France and Britain were struggling for their very existence.

By early afternoon the Plymouths and Dodges were unloaded. The horse meat and other commodities were all on trucks headed for the market places and stalls through which they were to be dispensed to merchants and consumers. Then the grating of chains told us that the anchors were being lifted. The pilots came alongside and took over and soon the ship was on its way to its final destination.

All afternoon we sloshed through the choppy waters of the English Channel headed for Britain's shore. By four o'clock the coast of England began to appear along the horizon. Cities and villages rose out of the sea. Irregular patchwork of fields, like a "crazy-patch" quilt, covered the hillsides. Tall chimneys, and rambling buildings told us that we were approaching a land of factories and mills as well as of farms.

By five o'clock when signs of evening began to appear we were sailing along the shores of the Isle of Wight. No more beautiful spot, they say, exists in all of Britain's domains than this lovely place with its Riviera climate, its natural beauty, and the traditional neighborliness that traces its origin back through the centuries and refuses to be spoiled by the rush and hurry of our time with all its modern contrivances that many of us think so essential for our comfort and welfare.

Near the shore—almost within calling distance, so it seemed —amid green trees and beautiful rolling fields stands the old, old Osborne Castle, a possession of the Royal Family. Since the days of the "Good Queen Bess" it has figured prominently in the affairs of England's kings and queens. It was here, historians tell us, that Disraeli delivered to Victoria the documents which made her the Empress of India. It's a lovely place, now no longer occupied but kept in repair. Cattle graze on the green sward up to the door through which once Royalty flowed. Church spires rise above the clumps of trees that shroud the villages, and "toll the knell of parting day" as they did centuries ago. All this and more give the land the air of peace and rest that the people say it really is.

When the sun was about to set, we came to a halt in the open sea. All around us were men-of-war, aircraft carriers, and destroyers that were moved away from the crowded docks and anchored safely against the day when England will need them again to defend her far-flung domain. One cruiser bore the American flag. Near it lay another that bore the British ensign and was decorated from stem to stern with flags, and pennants and colors that had little meaning to one who was unskilled and unlearned in the lore of the sea. When darkness fell she became a glare of light which shone from a multitude of incandescent lamps. When curious passengers interrogated the Americanized Englishman who sailed with us, as to the meaning of this display, he replied: "Hit 'as something to do wid the Queen, maybe 'er birthday." His knowl-

9

edge of Royal birth dates evidently had lapsed considerably and needed some refreshing. Sometime during the night when the water front was cleared, the ship resumed its journey and when the gong sounded in the morning we were alongside the dock and looked over the smoke-besmudged city of Southampton. After customs inspection by most obliging and courteous officials we set our feet on Britain's shore.

The boat train to London was very comfortable, and typically British. It carried us through villages and towns, over hills and through valleys covered with ripening grain or green with pastures filled with herds of cattle. Binders or combines, some drawn by tractors, were busy garnering the harvest. Then signs of London began to appear. This great, sprawling metropolis has had her place in the sun for centuries. Today she looked tired and worn —even the buildings have that appearance. Some of them still bear marks of the ravages of air raids. Others have had their "sores" mended and bravely rear their heroic heads again. In other places fine new structures have risen to replace those that went down during the war.

III

IN AND OUT
OF LONDON TOWN

London was old when William the Conqueror won the Battle of Hastings in 1066, and made himself master of Britain. In fact it already existed when Nero was lighting up his playgrounds with the burning bodies of the saints of the Roman Church in the latter half of the first century. The Norman invader must have been pleased with his newly acquired possessions for it is said that he exclaimed, "I will make England like the Garden of Eden and this city like the New Jerusalem."

Great and marvelous and wonderful as London is one looks in vain for the glory and splendor of the celestial city which John the Apostle describes in the Book of Revelation. That, however, does not mean that this greatest of all cities on the globe, mundane and earthly though it is, does not have a glory all its own. Its great buildings—cathedrals, government houses, banking institutions, market places, schools and universities, bookstalls, etc.—are seen on every hand. Subways, sometimes three deep or more, reach to all parts of the city. Escalators carry the multitudes from the surface to the railway system underneath the ground or bring them back again to where this mass of humanity is disgorged into the streets and thoroughfares of the world's greatest center of people.

The English revere and honor their kings and queens, their national heroes, and great men and women from every walk of life. Consequently, one sees an array of statuary stretching out in all directions along the streets, while plaques and other tokens of honor bedeck the walls and floors of many a shrine or other suitable place.

A trip to Buckingham Palace, in the heart of London, in time to see the colorful horse-guards change was the opening incident of an eventful day. At the entrance of the spacious grounds, on either side of the gateway, sit two mounted horsemen, mute and motionless as wooden men, resplendent in all the tinsel and trappings that go with their position. Their well-groomed mounts seem to have imbibed the spirit of their masters and are quite as unimpressed and unresponsive to attention. Along the stream that flows through the palace grounds are trees and shrubs and beds of flowers; and paths that lead to beauty spots which seem to have been designed to break the monotony of the seclusion which royalty has to bear.

One could not think of passing through this great sprawling metropolis without visiting Westminster Abbey and other noted shrines and places of devotion. Westminster is more than a place of worship. It is also the place where England's kings and queens receive their crowns amid impressive religious ceremonies. In a secluded place within the great building stands the simple wooden throne—not as imposing as an ordinary armchair—upon which the incoming monarch sits to receive the symbols of his office. One wonders who carved all the initials and names and designs on the seat and arms and sides—an exercise that reminds one for all the world of the work of the grade-school artists who left their names and other carvings inscribed on the classroom desks in the days some of us remember so well.

Underneath the seat of the throne is slung the famous "Stone of Scone" which the guide informed us is the identical one upon which Jacob rested his head the night after he left home to escape the consequences of his brother Esau's ire. Since that day in 1292 when Edward II made off with this "Stone of Destiny" this has been a matter of sore discontent among the Scotch who established the claim that:

> The nation of the Scots, free people
> If prophecy is not false,

Where this hoary pillar is found
There shall sovereignty have ground.

Of what value this "boulder" could be underneath the coronation chair is not easily comprehended, unless it is to serve as ballast to prevent a nervous king from "rocking the throne" while he is in the process of receiving the crown. What a position of power tradition holds when once it becomes thoroughly entrenched!

Westminster Abbey is a house of worship with its numerous little chapels where many of England's notables have found their last abode of rest. Gold incased effigies of kings and queens, nobles and warriors, lie atop the vaults where their mortal remains repose. Among them sleep others also of England's great statesmen, jurists, ministers, and lords. The ashes of some of them are interred underneath the stone slabs that cover the floor. Among them are the remains of David Livingstone—all except his heart which the Africans kept and buried underneath a tree in the far interior of that dark land as a token of the love they bore him. Each year thousands of travelers pause over the words he spoke in his loneliness in behalf of the people of that vast continent.

All I can add, in my solitude is, may Heaven's blessing come down on every one; American, Englishman, or Turk who shall help to heal this open sore of the world.

But there is another company of notables who were denied the honors and burial rites of the church. They are the nonconformists, the ones who broke with the ecclesiastical powers of the day and espoused the causes of righteousness and freedom that had too long been suppressed by the ecclesiastical powers. These found their last resting place in Bunhill, a cemetery that also carries in its bosom the mortal remains of one hundred and twenty thousand victims of the Black Plague which swept over western Europe and threatened to depopulate entire sections. It came from the Far East and followed the lanes of trade to Britain's shore. From thence it spread to the continent. Side by side with the plague victims lie the moldering bodies of these saints who were not considered worthy of a plot in "sacred" soil. Since that day these graves have become shrines before which people from many lands have stood with uncovered heads out of respect to the "unwanted Great" who sleep among the humble of the earth. These are they who broke through the clouds of superstition that shrouded their day and set aflame again the light of the Gospel which ushered in a new day.

Inscribed upon simple markers are names such as those of Susanna Wesley, mother of John and Charles, and Issac Watts, the hymn writer whose songs have filled the world with a melody of hope and joy that has given strength to the weary and faith to the halting. With them lies Joseph Hart whose song, "Come, Holy Spirit, Come," is still sung around the globe wherever Christians gather for worship. The simple epitaph engraved upon his headstone tells the story of his humble life:

Though I am a stranger to others, and a wonder to myself, Yet I know Him or rather am known of Him.

Here, too, lies John Bowring from whose pen came the immortal hymn, "In the Cross of Christ I Glory" and John Bunyan, author of *Pilgrim's Progress* which next to the Bible is perhaps the most widely read book in Christian circles. Among them, too, lies Daniel Defoe whose story of Robinson Crusoe has thrilled the hearts of many since his day. The frail marble slabs of these and a host of others are weathering in the wind and sun in strange contrast with those who were accorded a glorious burial as Britain's honored. However, since the heats and passions of that day have passed, some attempts have been made to atone for the wrongs done to these saints and a few of their names are now inscribed in Westminster Abbey's Hall of Fame.

But there are other cathedrals, churches, and places of worship in London. The Tabernacle where crowds gathered in Spurgeon's day still remains, but worshipers who grace its halls now represent but a shadow of the large multitudes that thronged the place when that great divine preached. Then there is St. Paul's with its array of saints and soldiery who sleep beneath its roof. Its beautiful altar and shrines cannot but leave a deep impression on all who come from across the world to behold this marvelous structure. The Westminster Chapel where G. Campbell Morgan held forth the Word of Life during his long and fruitful ministry is usually filled each Sunday morning with tourists. This no doubt is true because of the type of Gospel that is preached. Here I heard the noted Graham Scroggie deliver a powerful sermon on "The Passion of Our Lord"—a Baptist minister in a Free Congregational pulpit!

But a person will not have explored all the places of religious interest if he has missed the Sunday afternoon services and goings on at Hyde Park, of which our Boston Commons is a miniature replica. Here orators of every creed and doctrine from the most radical socioeconomic and political philosophies to the most liberal religious beliefs are expounded, including every shade and color between the extremes in every field of knowledge. Here you will learn why the people of Ireland ought to be united, why the Socialists should take over entirely the industries of England and why Communism should rule the world. Such a bedlam of voices one seldom hears, and yet each speaker, standing on his little platform, is far enough removed from the other so that the meetings go on peaceably.

Here where the largest crowd is, you will likely find that prince of preachers, Donald Soper of the Methodist church, an ardent Biblicist and advocate of Christian nonresistance. He speaks clearly and fearlessly and meets each question and issue fairly on the basis of the Scripture. Each Sunday afternoon at three o'clock he goes out Wesley-like dressed in a humble cassock, girded about with a leathern girdle, to where the multitudes are and preaches to them the "unsearchable riches" of Christ the Saviour of the world. When one thinks of all the unoccupied pews in the churches of London and around the world and then looks at the crowds on the Commons at Hyde Park, he is led to wonder whether perhaps the traditional manner of presenting the Gospel will have to give place to or at least be supplemented by other ways and means more primitive and less conventional if the masses are to hear the Good News.

Speaking about relics, one finds them in the museums of London. Here a person may lay eyes on the massive figures of lions, carved in stone, that once adorned the Palace gates at Nineveh in the day when Isaiah shook the Kingdom of Judah with his eloquence. Here, too, one may see a replica of the Stela containing the Code of Hammurabi by which the Babylonian Empire was governed at the time when Abraham was a lad playing on the street of Ur or in the fields, and along the banks of irrigating ditches adjoining the city. Or one may read, if he has mastered the language, a leaf from one of the most ancient of all the Greek manuscripts, the Codex Sinaiticus. A century ago the great Tischendorf found it in the monastery of St. Catharine at the foot of Sinai. Later it was transferred to St. Petersburg, Russia, where it lay until Russian Communism threatened to destroy every trace of religion in the Empire. Then England began negotiations for the purchase of this treasure. When once the $500,000 were paid, and it found its place in the museum of London, the world of Christian scholarship breathed easily once more. Days may be spent walking among the treasures of civilization and cultures, some of which were already ancient when Jacob bargained with Laban for his wives, but which painstaking, patient archaeologists have now recovered from the mounds and dust heaps of the world in which the patriarchs lived and wrought when the race was young.

One may spend weeks and months seeking out places of interest in this great city. A trip to the Tower of London is worth while if only to see the crown jewels and other amazing treasures that are here stored away under glass and heavily guarded, or to glance over the list of kings and queens who were deprived of their heads and brought to a premature end. Of if one is interested in antiquities he may include a visit to the old Roman wall, part of which has withstood the ravages of twenty centuries. As he gazes upon it he fancies he sees the galleys coming in from the

16

seven seas, unloading their cargoes of comfort, and luxuries brought from Rome and other markets of the world for the satisfaction of the officials who were then living in this outpost of Caesar's far-flung empire. Romans, Moors, Teutons, and other people from every section of the vast domain pass in imagination before one's eyes.

Coming back again to modern times we enter the high room overlooking Downing Street. Here six sedate and solemn men sit around a table piled high with legal tomes. It is a session of the Judicial Committee of the Privy Council, the court of last resort, the highest in the British Empire. The voice that speaks from here is theoretically an echo of the Monarch's voice that speaks from the steps of the throne. When the cry of "I appeal to Caesar" is raised in any part of the Empire, it is here where the cause is finally heard and where the last word is spoken for the four hundred million subjects that owe their allegiance to the British crown. No court ever existed with such wide jurisdictional powers. If the courts of Australia or New Zealand are not able to satisfactorily adjudicate the cause of sheep men or wool growers, or if a Canadian author is not satisfied with the ruling of the courts of the Dominion concerning a disputed manuscript, or if the African planter's contract for peanuts has been set aside or improperly construed by the local territorial Bench, the Privy Council gives the final, irrevocable decision from which there is no appeal. British officers of Justice in England and throughout the world have been drawn from the highest type of barristers within the nation, it is said, and are renowned for their incorruptible integrity.

Perhaps one should also stop to see the old Roman bath in the basement of a house at No. 5, Strand Lane. Two hundred years after Christ, some wealthy businessman, perhaps from the Mediterranean, had this place of ablution constructed for his homesick wife and her lady friends—so the guide imagined—who were experts in bathing and missed that luxury in this far-off place. It is sunken in the floor, fifteen feet long by six feet wide, built by a citizen of the only nation that ever understood bathing—so it is claimed. However, it seems to have lost the art since then. For seventeen centuries the stream that replenished the waters of this "tub" has been trickling from somewhere into what would seem to us like a swimming pool.

If one is down toward Billingsgate Market he can very well conclude that he is approaching the place where fish are sold. Here fishermen coming in from the seas with their haddock and plaice, and red-eyed herring, cod and skate, shrimp and shad, offer their smelly wares to a hungry public. At five o'clock in the morning a man with a peaked cap rings a large bell. Then the lights switch on and the bargaining begins. Buyers for restaurants, eating houses, markets, and shops are here inspecting the offerings that are on sale and poking their pudgy fingers into the flabby sides of these late inhabitants of the sea. As a person strolls among the stalls he is led to wonder whether anything can be as dead as a fish! Here the old guild—Worshipful Company of Fishmongers—still survives and its inspectors see that the quality of its wares is up to par and that business is conducted in accordance with its rules. There is lots of noise and confusion as the bargaining proceeds. The language, though not that of the drawing room, is refined, we were told, when compared with that of earlier years. In fact to say that people "Billingsgate" each other, was and is still synonymous with saying that they have attained the highest peak of development in the use of vile language and in the art of using sacred terminology in an irreverent way. The ripe, rich tang of the atmosphere that hangs over this place soon sends the novice on the way to where the air is seasoned with other scents save those of fish.

Madame Tussaud's Museum, containing the famous collection of life-size wax figures of the world's notables, is located in the heart of the city. It provides an admirable place to spend the days when the fog of winter or the showers of summer forbid outdoor sight-seeing. More than two hundred years ago a Swiss physician began making wax models of the diseased organs or limbs of his

18

patients. His success finally led him to abandon his profession and devote his time and skill to making figures of his friends. This grew into a large business and was finally moved to London. During the war the museum was closed but today it is again open after disastrous losses through fires and bombings. Standing on the museum floor, apart from the rest of her work, is the solitary figure of Madame Tussaud, the orphan girl whose lively imagination and deft fingers made her her uncle's assistant in the early days of his venture and found for her a place in the Royal Household of Louis XVI of France, where she taught the princess the art of wax modeling. After her uncle's death she came to England to display her wares and carry on her work. After years devoted to her profession, this deeply sincere and conscientious soul began to prepare herself for the last great event that comes to every living person. She turned over her business to her sons who had acquired her skill and love for the art. After other directions and admonitions she gave them her last words of counsel: "I implore you among all things—never quarrel."

A traveler will find it difficult to gain audience with the Royal family or with the top officials of most nations. He will have to travel many miles, across many countries to see the notables of the world—those of the United States, the Latin Americas, European countries, the Near and Far East, Africa and the Islands of the Sea. Here in this museum he will find them all, portrayed in figures cast in wax. They are dressed in real clothes. They appear so life-like and in such characteristic poses that one is almost moved to engage them in conversation. But this collection includes not only the famous but the infamous. In the dark recesses of the basement in what is known as the "Chamber of Horrors" one finds the images and figures of those who were in conflict with the law, base creatures drawn from the seamy side of life. They are the outcasts of society, broken men and women whom the world calls its "scum." Here, also, are duplications of prisons, instruments of torture, weapons, and machines of execution, among which is a guillotine accompanied by human heads in a basket.

A person would like to remain in London for weeks but the country is calling and one must be on the way. An excellent fleet of tourist busses, each carrying a guide well versed in British lore, leave the city each morning for various parts of the island. Our route took us out across the "Slough" once infested by robber bands that harassed the towns and villages as well as the country-side, and virtually claimed legal status for their profession. This road led to the Stoke Poges Country with its church and church-yard near by the Manor House of the William Penn family. Here by the old, old church, stills stands the yew tree, the marble slabs of the peasantry, the vaults of the nobility as they stood years ago when Gray wrote his *Elegy Written in a Country Churchyard.* Today as of yore,

> The curfew tolls the knell of parting day;
> The lowing herd winds slowly o'er the lea.
> Beneath those rugged elms, that yew-tree's shade,
> Where heaves the turf in many a mouldering heap,
> Each in his narrow cell forever laid,
> The rude forefathers of the hamlet sleep.

At Boulder's Lock the party left the busses for a steamer trip through the upper reaches of the beautiful Thames River to Windsor Castle. This royal residence was much occupied by one of England's most loved and greatest Queens—Victoria. Here the glory of Royalty is well preserved. Every boy or girl has no doubt sometime wondered what a home of kings and queens looks like. Here it may be seen. The canopied beds, the long dining room, the elaborate ball room and everything that pertains to royal life remains here undisturbed—except that the floor rugs are rolled up. With pride, maybe with some concessions, the guide pointed out to tourists from the United States the room in which President and Mrs. Wilson slept when they were en route to Versailles, where the great American idealist sat in an atmosphere that dripped with vengeance while a treaty was framed that was to make the world "safe for democracy." What a travesty!

Below Windsor Castle on a lonesome country road stands what

A village in rural England.

Westminster Abbey, London.

A Royal procession from Buckingham Palace.

Gutting Herring in England.

Stoke Poges Church, of the famous ELEGY WRITTEN IN A COUNTRY CHURCHYARD.

Bullange, Belgium, the village which the MCC unit helped to reconstruct.

Procession of the Penitentes, Belgium.

A typical peasant farm home, Luxembourg.

Interior of a peasant home, Luxembourg.

looks to us like a midwestern farm home. Here it is said the King and Queen found a quiet retreat where they are able to live a simple life which even royalty must often covet. On those occasions, so the guide said, the Queen donned her apron, cooked the meals, and kept the house. The King lounged with his shirt collar unbuttoned and smoked his pipe in peace while the princesses—in their days—romped and played on the lawn, barefooted.

The trail from Windsor to Hampton Court took us through historic country. The busses passed through Runnymede where the "freemen" exacted from stubborn King John, the Magna Charta which was the charter that eventually gave the English their liberty.

Hampton Courts, with its grounds and fountains patterned after those of Versailles, was the seat of the Tudor line of kings and queens to which the amorous and much married Henry VIII belonged. There too the "loving cousins" Elizabeth and Mary of Scotland, tradition says, spent much of their early lives, arranging "matches" for each other. However friendly or sincere these good offices were, they proved fruitless and the "good Queen Bess" spent all of her days in single blessedness. This was also the seat of the Hanoverian line when its rule began. Narratives of the time would indicate that the Britons as a whole did not look with favor on the induction of German princes to occupy the British throne. Even the great Walpole elaborated upon what seemed to have been a favorite theme of his day. He recalled his childhood impressions of Madame Schulenburg, later Duchess of Kendal, and Madame Kilmansegge, later Countess of Darlington. The latter he describes as an enormous figure as ample as the Duchess of Kendall was emaciated and long. "Two fierce black eyes," he says, "large and rolling, beneath two lofty arched eyebrows; two acres of cheek spread with crimson, an ocean of neck that overflowed and was not distinguishable from the lower part of her body, and no part restrained by stays." When the imported royalty went for outings the local populace amused itself by shouting rude remarks from secure distances. But the newly established

21

Hanoverians had their day also. One of their favorite pastimes, it is said, was to cut out paper caricatures of the English in which their distinguishing characteristics received sufficient overemphasis to furnish them amusement and to compensate as much as possible for the insults they had to bear.

The old home of the Royalty is now largely used for other purposes. One wing houses disabled soldiers and other parts are similarly used for benevolent projects. In passing out of the halls into the open grounds, the guide solemnly informed the women of our group that should any of them be here on All Saints night at two o'clock in the morning, they would see strolling on the veranda two decapitated ladies with their heads under their arms. What happened to the others—there seem to have been many—who lost their heads here no one seemed to know. Previous to the invasion of France President Eisenhower's headquarters were in the woods surrounding this palace. The barracks are still there, but the implements of war are gone. Peace, a quiet peace, now broods over the woods and meads—may it ever be so!

As we leave this lovely place the lines of Pope come to mind:

> Close by those meads, forever crowned with flowers,
> Where Thames with pride surveys his rising towers,
> There stands a structure of majestic frame,
> Which from the neighbouring Hampton takes its name.

One would like to linger in England, to travel over its winding roads that spread out over the countryside, to visit its lakes and streams and country villages and above all to become acquainted with its yeomanry secure in their simple homes. But time does not suffice and we must be on our way.

At the great, ornate Victoria Station the boat train stands waiting to take us to Dover from whence the ships will take us to new lands. So we bid England good-by. Land of streams of flowing water, of hills and valleys and homes of people, what a charming place you are! Farewell; Mother of Chaucer, and Shakespeare, of Pope and Shelley, Keats and Browning and

Wordsworth. What greatness you have given to the world! May the hand of a kindly Providence guide you in these troubled days, and may the greatness of your future rise above that of the past— benign Motherland that swaddled when it was an infant what has now become our homeland!

IV

ACROSS FLANDER'S FIELDS
AND LUXEMBOURG

In Flanders field the poppies grow
Between the crosses row on row.

All the way from Dover across the North Sea to Ostende our ship moved through the wreakage of war. The vessel was the last word in comfort, and glided easily across the choppy waters. The trip was sufficiently long to enable us to secure a good meal on board and gave us our first introduction to Belgian money. Here and there on every hand spars of sunken vessels rose above the surface and marked the graves of many a ship that came in line with missles of destruction, then floundered and sank to the bottom.

Belgium is a beautiful land consisting of what was formerly the Spanish Netherlands. It is a small country facing the North Sea. To those who are accustomed to the large farmsteads of the middle and western states of our own land, it looks like a garden which in reality it is. The population consists chiefly of Flemish people, who are akin to the Dutch, and the Wallons who are of French descent. The Flemish language is spoken in half of the provinces and the French in the other half, although the latter is understood everywhere.

Here the traveler who goes from England to Ostende receives his first view of Europe. The grain fields densely covered with stooks of wheat or other cereals, the carefully tilled patches of root crops, the long rows of flowers, bespeak a thrifty people. The diminutive threshing machines, the simple conveyances and farm machinery propelled by the large sorrel or roan Belgian horses, often alongside of an ox or milk cow, take one far back into the past and conjure up memories of an agricultural economy that has long since passed in the land where you and I live. One cannot but admire the patient toil of the peasant as he goes about his work, satisfied if he is but left alone to go his way in peace.

Belgium like other European countries bears deeply the scars of war. Before the ship reaches Ostende, the skeletons of buildings—roofless, windowless, and empty—stare at one as if in protest against intruders from foreign shores. Here on the continent the cities suffered the greater hardship during the years of the conflict. The quiet country homes seem to have been little disturbed by the raiding bombers that swept through the sky on their mission of destruction night after night, as well as day by day, though even here the marks of suffering are not altogether absent.

An afternoon ride from Ostende to Brussels took us through a beautiful country. Quaint villages dotted the landscape. Windmills flopped their wings in the breeze that swept the land and carried with it the coolness of the sea. How glad I was to get my first glimpse of continental Europe in the quietness and peace of rural Belgium! When the sun was low our train pulled into the station at Brussels. Travel in Europe is interesting. Not every family owns a car—in fact comparatively few do—and large numbers of people travel by train. A person may get at least a passing idea of life by observing the kind of folks that surround him as he sits in the comfortable coaches. For the most part they are a quiet, happy people who still enjoy their families, their friends, their homes and their land.

After considerable effort an English-speaking taxi driver—he thought he was speaking English, I was not too sure—was found and I was on the way to 6 Rue Jean Heymans where I was comfortably quartered at the Mennonite Central Committee headquarters during my stay in the city. David Derstine was in command here and Mrs. Derstine, a most gracious hostess, was in charge of the house.

Belgium, though a small land, is full of interest. The country like all of west continental Europe is full of refugees from the East, from Russia and the Balkan States, that have been drawn into the totalitarian orbit. How happy they would be to return to their fatherland were it possible to live anything like a life of peace! When one considers the extreme hardship these people undergo to escape from the way of living their homeland provides, he begins to realize the difficulties from which they must have fled.

Here I saw the first refugee camp. Many of them have lived for months, yea years, in these crowded quarters where there can be but little privacy, with rations, clothing, etc., sufficient only for the minimum requirements of their existence and yet within the bosom of these unwanted people there is still left a spark of the "hope that springs eternal." On the morning of my first visit to this place, several young wives with their children had just arrived and had been admitted. They were very happy with the prospect of getting to some place in the United States or Canada. Little, however, did they realize the bales of red tape that would need to be unraveled before such an event could take place. Nor did they know of the tedious interviews and long waits that so often resulted in disappointment until hope turns into despair.

Belgium was once the home of groups of Anabaptists as the records of Ghent disclose. Of chief interest in this ancient city is the Castle of the Count of Flanders, which dates back to the ninth century although the present structure was built in the twelfth century. Within this castle, like others of its time, there lived a self-contained household with its officers, retainers, servants, and possessions. Here during the Reformation the books of Luther were burned. Here at various dates Anabaptists were forced to recant, others by orders of the inquisition were decapitated, hanged, or smothered to death. Here are the underground dungeons where the heretics were imprisoned, and here too one finds the "torture chamber" together with its implements of cruelty with which they forced appropriate confessions from their victims in order to justify such inflictions as were deemed adequate punishment for the kind of people these dissenters from the faith were.

A trip to Vilvorde brought us to the spot where Tyndale, the great scholar and saint who set the style of language for our English Bible, was arrested for the crime of having translated the Scripture into a tongue which the people of his country could read. Having fled from England for safety from persecution he came finally to Antwerp where he settled down to the task of translating and printing Bibles which found their way back to the homeland in hogsheads labeled merchandise of various kinds. Unable to check the influx of what was considered pernicious and dangerous literature, the Bishop of London finally offered to buy all the copies which Tyndale had on hand in order to burn them and be done with the business forever. Being deeply in debt, he followed the advice of his friend and counselor, Packyngton, and sold out. When the deal was completed, the books delivered, and the money in hand, someone sagely remarked: "The Bishop has the Books, Packyngton has the thanks and Tyndale has the money." With the latter Tyndale paid his debt and with the balance he brought forth a new and better translation.

Finally this saintly scholar was betrayed into the hands of Bible-burners and executioners of translators and Bible readers. He suffered imprisonment at Vilvorde for sixteen months in a cold, dark cell. Out of the gloom of the prison comes the one remaining letter of all his correspondence addressed to the Marquis of Bergen-op-zoom in which he makes a touching request for clothing, books, and manuscripts that reminds one of the Apostle Paul's plea of II Tim. 4:13. Following is the letter:

I believe, right worshipful, that you are not ignorant of what has been determined concerning me; therefore, I entreat your lordship, and that by the Lord Jesus Christ, that if I am to remain here during the winter, you will request the procureur to be kind enough to send me from my goods in his possession, a warm cap, for I suffer extremely from cold in the head, being afflicted with a perpetual catarrh, which is considerably increased in the cell; a warmer coat also, for that which I have is very thin; also a piece of cloth to patch my leggings. My overcoat has been worn out. He has a woolen shirt of mine, if he will be kind enough to send it. I have also with him leggings of thicker cloth for putting on above; he has also warmer caps for wearing at night. I wish also his permission to have a candle in the evening for it is wearisome to sit alone in the dark. But above all, I beseech and entreat your clemency to be urgent with the procureur that he may kindly permit me to have my Hebrew Bible, Hebrew Grammar, and Hebrew Dictionary that I may spend my time with that study, and in return may you obtain your dearest wish, provided always it be consistent with the salvation of your soul. But if any other resolution has been come to concerning me, that I must remain during the whole winter, I shall be patient, abiding the will of God to the glory of the grace of my Lord Jesus Christ, whose spirit, I pray, may ever direct your heart. Amen.

—W. Tyndale

During the weary months of his confinement he was not forgotten by his friends, but their influence was not adequate to force his persecutors to surrender him whom they so bitterly hated. On October 6, 1536, in the midst of the crowded market place, surrounded no doubt by cowled and cassocked clergymen and dignitaries of the church, the noble saint was strangled and burned at the stake. The accounts rendered to the Lieutenant of the Castle show that the trial and execution of this great scholar and man of God cost the state the sum of 405 pounds. A poor investment, I would say!

Today there stands in what is a market place still, a simple shaft which marks the place where this martyr died. He is one of the heroes of faith, one of that noble company of scholars of whom the world was not worthy who came on the scene at a time of great need and helped to restore the Word of God to its rightful place among men.

In that little land stands another monument, a mound of earth with a lion on top, looking out across one of the most famous battlefields in Europe—Waterloo—where Napoleon's star of destiny set forever. On the walls of a large building overlooking the field where the conflict raged is a painting which reproduces the battle scene so well that one almost fancies he hears the cannon roar as they did on the fateful day when Europe was delivered from the power of one of the greatest military geniuses of modern times. As a child I often heard my forebears tell of the roads Napoleon built across the countries over which his armies moved, roads lined with trees on either side. Some of these are still in use daily and people now engaged in more peaceful occupations— when wars are over—sit in the shade and enjoy the fruit of his labors.

My wife recalls her mother's story of the day when her grandfather marched away with the "Little Corporal's" army on the ill-fated expedition to Moscow and left a bride of six weeks. She, the wife of such a brief time, like Sisera's mother "looked out at a window and cried through the lattice" into an empty future, "Why is his chariot so long in coming" (Judges 5:28)? Like that mother of old she found only words of comfort that had no meaning, except for the little son that came to keep alive the memory of a father who never returned nor was ever heard from.

On my last Sunday morning in Belgium, we held our worship privately in the Derstine home at the Mennonite Relief Committee Center. This being the anniversary of the day when Brussels was liberated by the English in 1944, the streets were gay with decorations and celebrating crowds of people. Public squares boomed with the voices of orators and happy groups displayed their joys in whatever way their fancy and means suggested or made possible.

At Bullange, a war wrecked village, a Mennonite Central Committee Unit of relief workers was stationed for a period of several years. As a token of good will this unit was engaged in restoring what had been destroyed during the war. Housed in a partly wrecked cheese factory from behind which once cannon roared, they rebuilt a number of homes for people who would otherwise not have been able to have their living quarters renewed. Not only did they restore buildings but they also laid the foundation of hope in the hearts of many for whom the future seemed so empty. For long years the names of those strangers who came from across the sea will not be forgotten and the kind help rendered in the time of need will no doubt live on in the hearts of new generations as the story is told around their firesides.

En route to Luxembourg is located the cemetery where the American boys, victims of the Malmay Massacre, lie sleeping. One morning a moving column of United States soldiers unexpectedly encountered a superior number of the enemy on this spot and after having surrendered they were shot. The spot where this tragedy took place is now enclosed with a stone wall above which floats the American flag while o'er the graves and around the walls the peaceful heather grows. What horrors occurred where now the peaceful winds sigh and warming rays of the sun coax forth a meager life to heal the wounds of war!

Farewell, Belgium, we leave you now, brave little land.

> Gold and green are your fields in peace,
> Red have they been in war.
> Black are they when the cannon cease
> Then white forever more.

Long have been your days of sorrow and suffering. May your wounds be speedily healed and may the fields of white, "with their crosses row on row" be undisturbed forevermore!

From Belgium the road led through the little duchy of Luxembourg, a tiny little state in the Rhine country. Here we saw the rolling hills covered with grain and herds of cattle. Near the top of one of the low mountains we happened upon a lonely shepherd with his faithful collie and flock of sheep. What a lovely setting! The trees that lined the roads through the forest were painted white to guide the army transports that during the war moved without lights after darkness covered the earth. Further on we passed by the ruins of Kipperhof where Bishop Joseph Oesch lived before General Patton's army stormed through the country and reduced the old, old place with its extensive buildings to a mass of rubble that thus far has not been rebuilt. A night with one of the Oesch families brought us in touch with the hospitality of the Luxembourg Mennonites. How gracious they are—brethren in the Lord indeed, who in their isolation are hungering for fellowship and spiritual food to live by! The farmstead is patterned after the European style. An ample dwelling house close by the large, ancient stone dairy barn, set in the midst of broad fields, is an appropriate setting in which one may observe the farm life of that country.

Beyond the city of Luxembourg is located the cemetery where lie buried the men of Patton's army who fell when he swept across the country into Germany, and left behind him a trail of ashes and a scorched and blasted earth. Row on row of white crosses stretch across the acres and acres of beautifully landscaped burial ground where:

> The muffled drum's sad roll has beat
> The soldier's last tatoo.

On a little eminence facing the lines of white markers is the simple monument that marks the grave of the General himself who survived the war only to go to his death in an automobile accident after the conflict was over. One comes away from such scenes with a deep feeling of depression. When will the world become wise enough to learn to settle its problems without making it necessary to waste life and property through warfare in order to accomplish its aims? Here behind the whitened crosses or under the Stars of Bethlehem lie those who once were full of life and hope as all young people are. They dreamed of love and home, playing children and peaceful firesides. They too wanted to live as all other people do. Now because of conditions which they themselves did not create they lie in burial grounds such as this around the world. The simple, lovely markers line on line, the flowers that bloom over their graves, the inscriptions, however eloquent or touching, mean nothing to them now. They are dead and all their longings and aspirations are at an end. How

31

long, how long will it be till the nations learn! May we hope that the day will ever come when men will have grown big and wise and honest enough to lay aside all selfishness and littleness, and avarice, and jealousy and seek to justly and equitably settle the problems of nations as they settle their own?

V

THE ALSATIAN LAND
AND LORRAINE

The Alsatian land is a little island of culture, pretty much its own, that lies between the French on the one side, the Germans on the other and the Swiss at the upper end. It stretches along the Rhine from the Swiss border to Luxembourg from whence Lorraine turns its toe westward to its border beyond the city of Metz. In size it consists of some five thousand six hundred square miles with a population of two to three million souls. Topographically nature has been good to it. Low hills extend from the Vosges Mountains on the east and give it a charm all its own. Streams that have their source in the adjoining highlands flow through the valleys and not only add to the attractiveness of the landscape but furnish the power to turn the wheels of its mills and factories.

Agriculture is still the most important of all its industries and under the skilled hand of its husbandmen its soil yields abundant harvests of grain and other crops. But the country is not void of other resources. Between Hagnenau and Wissembourg is found the largest oil field in France. Its mines yield salt, potash, coal, and iron ore. Textile mills, steel and iron works as well as many of the smaller crafts and trades are found scattered throughout the country. Its beautiful, fertile land is coveted by its neighbors on either side and has been the "bone of contention" between them for centuries. I don't blame them! Here on its soil the American armies first met the Germans during the first World War, and here the first American boys fell and lie buried—the

33

first one an Iowa lad. Someone has called Lorraine the most beautiful cemetery in the world. No one knows how many casualties lie buried in its bosom as a result of the wars that raged within its borders since Julius Caesar conquered these parts years before the Prince of Peace was born.

Long ago, in 58 B.C., the inhabitants of these regions suffered at the hands of this conquering hero when he added to his laurels the conquest of Gaul which as every high school student knows "was divided into three parts." No one expected then that he, the High Marshal of the legions of Rome, would also invade the high school curriculum of our day and bring into bondage the thousands of students as they try to conquer the language of the History of Caesar's Gallic Wars. May peace brood over the ashes of their failures!

Along about the middle of the first century B.C. Caesar met and defeated a Germanic tribe that had crossed the Rhine near the River Neckar and had taken possession of what is now Alsace. The decisive clash took place at a town named Ochsenfeld in which the Roman Eagles prevailed and this sector of the world became a part of the Empire. For four centuries the Caesars ruled the turbulent and freedom-loving Alemanni. Even after the battle of Strassbourg the discontent of the Germanic and Frankish tribes continued until Attila, the terrible Hun, with his brutal hordes, appeared on the horizon. Then all of them united their forces to block the way of this ruthless invader. The final conflict that checked his encroachment upon this section took place at Chalons in 451. Relieved from this threat the Allemanni, a Germanic tribe, took advantage of the declining power of their conquerors and occupied what is now Alsace-Lorraine and gave to the country the language and culture which it has retained to this day.

But the struggle was not over. A spot so beautiful, productive, and favorably located was not easily overlooked by lords and kings with covetous eyes. Charlemagne made it a part of the

Holy Roman Empire which history indicates was not Roman and could hardly have been called holy when considered in terms of all that happened under the guidance and control of the Emperor and his successors. In those days the seat of the government and the royal residence was established successively at such cities as Schlettstadt and Colmar where the ruler basked in the beauty of his surroundings and, no doubt, lived on the fruits of this lovely country.

But these Alsatians are devotedly loyal to their land and their culture. In language they have a dialect whose basis is German and in origin they are probably Germanic. In sympathy they are French and prefer to be under French domination. In his comments in the Encyclopædia Britannica Dr. J. C. Meyer, Professor of History, Western Reserve University, gives the following characterization of these remarkable people. He says:

Great scholars have attempted to prove that the natives belong to the French or the German nationality. The careful observer who speaks and understands the dialect and who listens to the conversations of the natives whether in their homeland, in the Alsatian Cafe in Paris or in groups of exiles or immigrants from the region, is likely to conclude after hearing them speak only less condescendingly of the Franzos (Frenchman) than of the Schwob (German), that the Alsatian is above all an Alsatian. . . . The attendant in the museum or in the library unconsciously makes a distinction between what is Alsatian and what is French and German. The average native suffers from what is an inordinate local pride and is possessed of a wealth of local tradition, some of which antedates French and German nationalism by a millennium. Important in that tradition is the love for liberty and the spirit of political and economic democracy which neither the French nor German statesmen seem able to comprehend. By the Swiss it is taken for granted. Religion has long had a prominent place in the life of the people. Louis XIV, the Napoleons, and Bismarck learned to respect these traditions, but sometimes lesser statesmen have shown less wisdom.

It was here in this land that Anabaptism took root. From here the liberty-loving folks that were out of accord with their neighbors on the question of faith, came to America and founded the large settlements in Ohio, Illinois, and other places throughout the United States and Canada. In America their spirit remains the same. Their convictions are deep and their nature unyielding in matters where their rights and privileges are involved. They have been a bulwark against any influences and trends that tend to deprive them of their liberty and the freedom to manage their own affairs for themselves.

It was from the life and experience of these people who were often tossed hither and yon by marching armies that Goethe drew some of the characters and materials for his scenes in the beautiful story of Hermann and Dorothea when these folks fled from their country during the Revolution of 1792-94.

Here too Longfellow found his material for the Cobbler's Story in his *Tales of the Wayside Inn.*

> I trust, he says, that somewhere, somehow
> You all have heard of Hagenau.
> A quiet, quaint and ancient town
> Among the green Alsatian hills,
> A place of valleys, streams and mills.
>
> It happened that in the good old times,
> While yet the Meister-singers filled
> The noisy workshop and the guild
> With various melodies and rhymes,
> That here in Hagenau there dwelt
> A cobbler—one who loved debate
> And arguing from a postulate
> Would say what others only felt.
> A man of forecast and of thrift,
> And of a shrewd and careful mind
> In this world's business, but inclined
> Somewhat to let the next one drift.

It so happened that this Alsatian cobbler's wife had made provision for her eternal welfare by the purchase of proper indulgences from the notorious Tetzel who had set Luther's ire

aflame by his unholy dealing with people's souls. When this good
wife died her husband ignored the services of the church until
the village padre in company with a notary called to remind
him of his duty and incidentally collect something for the coffers
of the church. Then pressing his case, the priest said:

> . . . and hath mass been said
> For the salvation of her soul?
> Come speak the truth! Confess the whole.
>
> The cobbler without pause replied:
> "Of mass there was no need
> For at the moment when she died
> Her soul was with the glorified!"
> And from his pocket with all speed
> He drew the priestly title-deed
> And prayed the Justice he would read.
>
> The Justice read amused, amazed;
> And as he read his mirth increased.
> At times his shaggy brow he raised,
> Now wondering at the cobbler gazed
> Now archly at the angry priest.
>
> "From all excesses, sins and crimes
> Thou hast committed in past times,
> I thee absolve,
> So that in dying unto thee
> The gates of heaven should open be!
> Though long thou livest, yet this grace
> Until the moment of thy death
> Unchangeable continueth."
>
> Then said the Priest: "I find
> This document duly syned
> Brother John Tetzel, his own hand
> At all tribunals of the land
> In evidence may be used,
> Therefore, acquitted is the accused."
> Then to the cobbler turned my friend
> "Pray tell me, didst thou ever read

Reynard the Fox?"—"Oh, yes, indeed!"
"I thought so. Don't forget the end."*

Alsatian ghost stories are famous and others such as the one just quoted, express the delightful wit of these good folks.

"On the broad, drowsy land below" stands Hagenau—an old, old city in the midst of its beautiful hop fields which here as elsewhere lend color to the countryside. The "shadowy forest filled with game" covering some thirty-two thousand acres was evidently at one time more than a wooded area. It was a large burial ground dating back—probably—to Celtic times. It is said to contain more than five hundred mounds identified as abodes of the dead. Europe's population beneath the ground, no doubt, far outnumbers that which is above it.

The exploration of this forest was forced upon us one night when a worn-out fan belt delayed a Volks-wagen of the Hitler vintage, overloaded with Americans en route to a conference of relief workers in Germany. This brought us to the edge of the forest after dark. A tap on the doorbell of a long, rambling, barrackslike building brought a white-robed sister of some religious order to the window of the second floor. When she found herself confronted by a man she withdrew and sent a "lay-woman" to answer inquiries. She graciously gave us directions regarding the way to Wissembourg. At the place where the road divides our combined judgment failed us and our little Volks-wagen clattered down the wrong trail. The most serious objection to this error was the utter darkness which prevented us from seeing what is reputed to be a lovely forest. After having explored what seemed the entire area, some good farmer folk directed us to our destination. European cities—especially the smaller ones—are not aglare with lights and neon signs as are those we are accustomed to. After having added Wissembourg to our explorations of the night a man at the city electric plant directed us to the Children's Home at Weiler.

---

* Adapted from Longfellow's *Tales of the Wayside Inn*.

In this section are found the cheerful villages—the most picturesque in Europe—with their winding streets and houses of gay designs. Strassburg stands astride the crossroads of the country. It is a river port with a population of more than two hundred thousand. Its red sandstone cathedral with its spire rising four hundred and fifty feet above the street is said to be one of the most audacious in all of Europe. Its astronomical clock is a scientific curiosity. Every hour it places on parade a number of amusing allegorical figures to the great delight of children, tourists, and travelers. Here Gutenberg perfected his printing press and Pasteur, the great scientist, taught chemistry in its university. Here, too the "Marseillaise" was composed in 1792. From this goodly land came refugees in the early history of our nation when the struggle between France and Germany was hot. Among the hired men employed in our neighborhood in the days of my childhood was one of the sons of this beautiful country who entertained us children with songs of his beloved Strassburg and the hills of Alsace. No doubt memories of his family, the villages, and the happy people he once knew were in his mind as his moods became more solemn while he sang again the folksongs of the homeland he loved:

> Es, es, es, und es, es ist ein schweren Schlusz
> Weil, weil, weil und weil ich nach Frankreich muss,
> Drum schlag ich Strasbourg aus mein Sinn
> Und wende mich Gott weiss wo hin.
> Ich muss mein Gluck probieren
> Marschiren!

In this section of the country, in one of its quaintest and most lovely villages is the home of a former student of Goshen College. Here, too, are the Geisberg and Lembach communities known to our spiritual kinsmen, that were thrice overrun with contending armies and as many times evacuated and blasted out of existence. When I saw these places new buildings were rising again and life was going on. Here are also located the cities and towns of Colmar and Belfort, Altkirch and Mulhouse from whence earlier some of our ancestors came who built up their thrifty, flourishing settlements in America and where today groups of them still remain.

When I last passed through Alsace it rained. The hop fields surrounding Hagenau dripped with moisture but behind the clouds the bright sun of the Alsatian land shone ready to break forth and show up its hills and valleys, its villages and cities, its farms and homes in their most glorious array.

VI

CHARMING SWITZERLAND

Switzerland, mother of Conrad Grebel, Felix Manz, Andrew Castleberger, George Blaurock and William Reublin, we salute you! Here in your land a faith was reborn that set in motion wide new movements in the world and released the Gospel from a bondage that had lasted for centuries. In your soil, impregnated with the spirit of freedom, great souls planted the seeds of the Christian liberty which brought forth its fullest fruit in the faith of the Swiss Brethren. At a time when the powers of the church and state were against them, this group of believers courageously rejected the large body of ecclesiastical tradition that had grown up through the centuries, as well as the whole state-church system. The movement became known as Antipedobaptist or Anabaptist because its founders and leaders repudiated the doctrine of infant baptism and insisted that the rite should be administered only upon a personal confession of faith and acceptance of Jesus Christ as Saviour. They accepted the Scripture as the final authority in all affairs pertaining to faith and life. Holy living and a humble denial of self was practiced in all matters in which their own desires came into conflict with the Word of God.

The stubborn persistence of these humble folk and their unflinching loyalty to these convictions set the fires of persecution burning and caused them much suffering and hardship; often imprisonment, exile, and death. It was not until the warm breath of freedom swept over the world early in the nineteenth century that liberty finally came to these patient souls.

Switzerland, brave little land, maintained, not without anxiety and difficulty, its neutrality and freedom during two global wars that rocked the world in this present century and robbed many lands and people of the liberty that had earlier been dearly bought. It is cut off from the sea on all sides, except for the streams that flow past its doorway or which have their sources in the icecaps or snowfields that lie upon its mountain peaks. It is a broken, mountainous country, with beautiful valleys filled with villages and towns and lovely homes such as the Swiss know how to make.

The importance of Switzerland is not related in any way to its size. In fact, it is important in spite of its size. In length it measures only two hundred ten miles. Its breadth is approximately half that distance. It consists of twenty-five political divisions known as cantons or demicantons.

By its constitution adopted in 1848, it became a confederation of states or cantons. In 1874, this fundamental law was revised and it became a Federal State, governed by an assembly of one hundred eighty-nine deputies which are elected by popular vote. The executive power of the nation is vested in an Executive Council, consisting of seven members, chosen for a term of three years by the National Assembly. The members of this Council are heads of the administrative departments of the government which correspond somewhat to the cabinet officers which the President of our country appoints. The President and Vice-President of this body are the Chief Magistrates of the Republic and hold their respective offices for a term of one year. The General Assembly is the law-making body and concerns itself chiefly with such duties. The investigation of its crooks, gamblers, law breakers, traitors and public scoundrels is left largely to the Department of Justice and the judicial system which has been set up for their trial and prosecution.

After a long struggle covering centuries, the people of Switzerland were finally granted complete religious liberty by the constitution of 1874. It was here that the seeds planted by Grebel and his followers more than four hundred years before reached their full fruitage. By this same act a number of powers were taken out of the hands of the church. Civil marriage is now compulsory. Jesuit Societies are excluded and the establishment of new convents is prohibited. The church may appoint no bishop except by sanction of the government.

Few countries the size of Switzerland can boast of such a wide variety of climate and vegetation as can this little mountain-crowned republic. In the lower altitudes, the vineyards prosper and the wineries flourish. From here, the grapes as well as the wines find their way to markets of cities and towns. Beyond the vine-clad hills lie the clumps or rows of walnut trees and fields of spelt which, farther on, blend into groves of lovely birches, and grains such as oats and barley which stretch onward to the upper fringes of pines and maples. Then come the Alpine pastures where herdsmen graze their cattle during the brief summer months. From here they carry their cheese and other dairy products down the mountain trails to where the motors run and from thence they find their way to the consumer's table.

In the fields of industry one finds the famed Swiss watches and clocks, laces and embroideries as well as other needlework, wood carvings and such other products as the patient skill of these industrious people produces. The name "Gerber" is to the cheese industry of Switzerland what "Kraft" is to America. Dairy products and fine candies of the choicest kind are manufactured here, much of which finds its way to markets far beyond the borders of its homeland. Swiss watches were on sale at Aden when we stopped there en route to India and Swiss chocolates could be bought in Bombay.

As one travels from place to place he becomes impressed with the tremendous electrical development of the country. Deep mountain gorges furnish the power to turn the generators which supply the electricity for the factories and mills, the trams and trains throughout the country, and the lights that brighten the homes and streets of the cities.

The Swiss people are a lovely folk, industrious, intelligent and skillful. They are kind, considerate and clean, good house-keepers and good cooks. One feels at home here and could easily stay with them always. Even the Hindu boy whose upbringing, way of life, and religion were as different from that of central Europe, as the world is wide, after having spent four years at the University of Basel, wished that he could stay in Switzerland the rest of his days.

The population is mixed in race and language. German is spoken by a majority of the people in fifteen of its cantons, French in five and Italian in one. To a person who comes from a large country whose domain stretches over thousands of miles with a state owned and controlled educational system and only one language spoken throughout its entire length and breadth, it seems strange to find in a nation so small, the sectional differences that exist here. One may presume that long ago when mountain barriers were not as passable as they are now, the inhabitants of each valley developed along its own lines and built up a loyalty to its own ways that is not easily overcome.

But Switzerland has other things to sell besides watches and cuckoo clocks, cheese, and other wares that are the product of her mills and factories. It has its scenery, a commodity—if such it may be called—that has been sold to admiring travelers for centuries and still has all of it left. These folks know not only how to package and display their dairy and other products to the best advantage, they know also how to show up their mountains and hills and valleys in order to allure nature-loving folks that travel across the world to seek out and admire its wonders. Winding roads, such as only highland engineers know how to build, traverse mountains piled one upon the other with deep gorges and gaping chasms between. Large busses driven by expert operators follow the highroads to the farthest divide where one becomes enthralled with the grandeur of this Garden of God.

Here the glaciers have their home, from which issue rivers

44

and streams that furnish the power which sends her finely equipped, government-owned trains speeding across the country to all its borders and beyond. From these snowy heights come also the waters that fill the lakes whose shores are studded with villages and towns that are the delight of travelers and sight-seers from many lands. In the beautiful valleys that lie between are found the homes of the husbandry which adorn the landscape and add to its impressive and unforgettable beauty.

A person who has once entered Switzerland would hardly dare to return to his homeland without having spent some time traveling over its mountains, across its lakes, and through its valleys. Accordingly, I left the Mennonite Central Committee headquarters at Basel early one September morning for a week or ten days' vacation. The long, beautiful, international train stood at the station when I arrived, waiting to take on its load of passengers. Promptly, on the second so it seemed, the wheels began to roll. We were on our way for a period of happy, pleasant, thrilling experiences on the rails, through endless tunnels and then on to lakes, rivers and cities.

The country itself is beautiful and it seems that the people and what they have added makes it all the more charming. Lovely Swiss homes dot the valleys or hang—often precariously —on the mountainside where they may be reached by winding trails that play hide-and-seek with the observer as he floats smoothly along on the speeding train. It was the time of the year when farmers were occupied with seasonal duties. Many a scythe, swung by lusty arms, clipped the succulent grasses that grew in their narrow fields while small wagons, drawn by oxen, gathered up the hay and hauled it to the feeding stall or stored it in barns that were frequently joined to the living quarters of the family. In the lower altitudes most luscious grapes were being garnered for the wineries or for the shops and markets of the villages, cities and towns.

The first stop was at Zurich, the seat of a great University and the scene of many a tragedy during Switzerland's struggle for religious freedom. Fortunately, the hotel where I stayed was in an historic part of the city. From my window I could see the Grossmünster Church where Zwingli and Bullinger held their famed disputations with Grebel, Manz, and Blaurock. Close by the hotel flowed the River Limmat where Manz was drowned. Along this street Blaurock was driven with hands tied behind his back, stripped to the waist, and beaten with rods until the blood flowed. Referring to this incident in later years, Zwingli says that Blaurock was so badly abused he was brought near to the gates of Hades. But it can hardly be said that those who appeared to be the victors were always victorious. After the above unhappy episode one of Zwingli's supporters wrote anxiously from Strassburg inquiring about the fate of these unfortunate victims. He says: "It is reported here that Felix Manz of your city has suffered death and died gloriously," and added that Zwingli's cause had suffered greatly on that account.

The University was not in session. Some students remained and were eager to give information and show an American what a European university looks like. The Grossmünster Church was closed but the inscriptions and a few plaques on the outside furnished some information that was desired.

At the close of a drizzly afternoon the skies cleared, the full moon rose and lighted up the city and the surrounding hills. Through the open window my eyes followed the street and stream up toward the church where the famed disputations were once held, but my thoughts wandered far back into the past. I almost fancied that I saw the "shades" of the saints of long ago coming out of the dark recesses, where their places of worship may once have been hidden, and creep silently along in the shadows toward their homes. Places like this, once so filled with tragedy, conjure up strange thoughts! This evening everything seemed so peaceful and quiet that one could hardly imagine that once it was filled with sorrow.

The next day found us en route to Lucerne and across the lake of William Tell fame. How smoothly these steamers, filled with happy folks, glide over the waters, and how restful it is! At each village where stops were made people whom we had met came and went. These acquaintances for such short duration drop out of our presence and will perhaps appear no more except as they come into our memories in the years ahead. High above us on the mountainsides were little specks that marked the homes of the herdsmen who take their cattle to the summer pastures on these remote heights where the clouds are always low. Even the holiday passengers with whom we sailed seemed subdued in the midst of such sublime surroundings and grandeur. In the midst of the peace and quietness hardly a sound was heard save the churning propellers and now and then the tinkling of an Alpine bell, or the blast from the long horn of the cowherd that echoed from mountainside to mountainside across the waters.

Late in the afternoon we left the boat and took the train at Fluelen to Gösehenen from whence we were carried up the steep incline by cog-train to Andermatt where the air is rare and the nights are cool even during the hot summer season. Here was a restful little hotel—good food, good company, and a deep feather bed to keep one warm during the chilly night. Early in the morning before the sun rose above the peaks a "tap" at the door awakened us and with a friendly voice informed us that breakfast was waiting. The tinkling of bells told us that the cattle of the high hills had been milked and were on their way to pasture. A blast from a long horn announced the arrival of the bus.

This was destined to be a day of thrills. Owing to the lateness of the season most of the tourists were gone, hence there was lots of room. When the bus drove away from the station at Andermatt what few passengers there were thought perhaps we were near the top of Switzerland. But still we climbed upward where the road wound and curved and seemed at times to have a slender hold on the very steep hillsides to which it clung. Now and then we suddenly looked into empty spaces where the driver hit curves so short that it appeared as though he was driving off into the "blue." At one of those turns there was a sign saying, "Hier ist Peter—verunglückt." When my eyes followed the steep declivity down which his body must have rolled, I concluded that Peter did not only have an accident—he, no doubt, provided the occasion for a very sad meeting at the village church.

The trip took us upward to where the glaciers are born. The Rhone River has its source in such a place at a turn in the road where the bus stopped at a lovely restaurant for rest and lunch. Then the trail led down a long, steep grade to a beautiful flower-bedecked village from which we climbed again to greater heights where the falling mist told us that we were in the clouds. Once during the day, kind nature drew aside her flimsy curtain and unveiled the Jungfrau with the white cap which she wears on her stormy head the year around. Our route took us through sunshine and rain, past vast power plants located in deep recesses, and large summer hotels to which people come from around the world for rest and quietness on these sublime heights where ragged nerves are soothed and jaded spirits are made new.

At Meiringen the passengers left the bus and trains carried them to Interlaken where markets and shops and ancient things afforded one ample opportunity to pass the time interestingly and where wares of all kinds, for which this place is noted, tempted one to part with his money. In the middle of the river that flows by, stands an old round tower with its dungeon far below the water level of the stream. Here, in this gloomy place, so a flower vendor informed us, is where they kept their heretics and Anabaptists when imprisonment and extermination were still in vogue. The devices of the Inquisitors had surely reached a high state of development during those days when the ax, the guillotine, drowning, and flames were used as means of settling their ecclesiastical problems.

From Interlaken, a steamboat carried us over Thunersee to Thun from whence a swift train took us to Bern, the capital city of the country, where a restful hotel awaited us. Bern is a beautiful city with its great government buildings, lovely parks, shops, street markets and some industries of a refined nature, one of the park bench occupants informed me. By this, he may have meant such as would not profane the beauty of the place with grime and noises.

After restful days at this beautiful place we were on the train again en route to Lausanne by Lac (Lake) Lemon which Byron in his travels said:

> . . . Woos me with its crystal face.

A pleasant afternoon with new friends on the lake steamer came to a close when the sun went down over the city of Geneva, the home of the League of Nations. This is a historic spot. Here John Calvin, lawyer, theologian, and man of letters lived and wrought in Reformation times and by his rigid enforcement of righteous principles, based on the Scriptures, turned the disorderly populace of low morals and rowdyism into a quiet and peaceable people.

Geneva became, also, a sort of a "city of refuge" for such men as the great John Knox of Scotland during the time when the "Bloody Mary" tried to bring Britain's populace back into the fold of the Roman Church. Here he formed a rich and congenial fellowship with the persecuted refugees from Holland, Germany, France, and other lands where they were beset on every hand by dangers because of their faith. In this city these unwanted intellectuals thrived in the atmosphere created by the scholarly, dispeptic Calvin. From the academy operated here came an array of learned, devout, fearless ministers who became leaders in the Reformation movement and champions of Protestantism wherever they went. Out of this stronghold came, too, the doctrines which colored the beliefs of several of the strong churches and set the pattern of their government.

On Sunday morning early, I walked to the docks for a last glimpse of:

> Clear, placid Lemon! The contrasted lake,
> With the wide world I dwelt in, is a thing
> Which warns me with its stillness to forsake,
> Earth's troubled waters for a purer spring.

A train ride from Geneva to the Italian border brought my vacation in Switzerland to its close, but the quarters of the Mennonite Central Committee at Basel were still my European home. To this place my travels brought me again several times before I left the continent but my stays were brief and from henceforth my journeys were made for other purposes than those of sight-seeing and recreation.

Though Switzerland kept itself out of the last two great wars it does not mean that it had no anxious moments as, for example, when an American bomber accidentally dropped his missiles of destruction within its borders. Nor does it mean that being drawn into the conflict was beyond a possibility. Its vulnerable points bristle with antiaircraft guns, and weapons of defense of all kinds. Its mountains overlooking highways, and passes, railroads and other points where invasions might be attempted by land or air are strongly fortified and prepared to resist any effort of the foe to secure a foothold on its soil. Deep within the heart of the high peaks and other advantageous and inaccessible places in the mountains are large chambers excavated by engineers where thousands of soldiers may be quartered in wartime. Here guns and other implements of war are mounted and ready, they say, for any emergency. Here also is stored food in sufficient quantities to sustain a beleaguered garrison for months, even years, in case help from the outside should be cut off. So cleverly are these places designed to fit into the landscape that they are barely discernible, in some instances not at all. On arriving at one of the passes we barely took notice of the large boulders that lay strewn on the slopes around us as they are everywhere in these

50

great hills. On closer observation we discovered that they were not rocks at all but antiaircraft shelters with guns poking their ugly noses from underneath.

When one looks at all the bunkers and walls, tunnels and entanglements of the Maginot and Siegfried Lines and recalls the boast of their impregnability, he is made to wonder about the trustworthiness of any such provision that man may make. We know now that they were not adequate to prevent armies from moving hither and yon in their maneuvers of war. Usually the ingenuity of man can overcome any obstacles he may create. And above all this, there is a Hand which holds a power that knows no limit and a Mind that knows how to bring to naught every device of man's creation. When humanity has done its best—or its worst—to bring about its designs and accomplish its ambitions then that *Great Immeasurable Power* from whose presence there is no escape begins to move and the glory of man's achievements fades away. Did not such a simple, common occurrence as a snow storm lay low Napoleon's hosts and bring to naught at Moscow his designs upon Russia—or a rain in Flanders bring to an end at Waterloo his plans for an Empire? Someday the voice that *roared* out of Zion in Amos' day will speak again. Then the things that can be shaken will be removed and those that can not be shaken will remain.

My days in charming Switzerland were done. With regret I left the place but memories of it will linger with me always. It has been a pleasant host and has much to teach us. While wars raged around it even to its very gates, it remained an island of peace and a haven of refuge in a wide, storm-tossed sea of madness and strife. May He who rules the destiny of the nations ever keep it in peace though the waters thereof roar and its mountains be carried into the midst of the sea. This little land is blessed of God with amazing beauty and loveliness! Though the fires of its persecution burned long and their flames were hot, we love it still. Many a saint who died for his faith lies enfolded in its bosom. Other thousands who fled those dire days found homes in a new world where they brought forth strong settlements which bear the names of the places which they left— Berne, Sonnenberg, etc. The germ of freedom that stirred its soul in the early Reformation days has now brought forth its full, rich, fruit—liberty to follow one's conscience in all things that pertain to faith and life. May you, charming land and lovely people, always abide in peace—the peace you so dearly bought. *Amen.*

VII

SUNNY ITALY

Italia! oh Italia! Thou who hast
The fatal gift of beauty, which became
A funeral dower of present woes and past—
On thy sweet brow is sorrow ploughed by shame
And annals graved in characters of flame.

   * * *

Then might'st thou more appeal—or less desired
Be homely and be peaceful, undeplored
For thy destructive charms.

TRAVELING TO ROME

These lines from Byron, hidden somewhere in the recesses of my subconsciousness, rose in my mind when for the first time the land of Italy, like the form of an Enchantress, began to unveil itself before my eyes. It is a land renowned for its lovely climate, its charming, romantic people, its great cities, cathedrals, and works of art, the greatest of which have their origin in the past and are but remnants of the glory of the days that are gone.

Genoa, home of Christopher Columbus, provided shelter for me the first night after we crossed the Swiss border into Italy. What a thrill to look out of the hotel window and see the first rays of the rising sun light up the statue of the Genoese sailor who dared to believe that the world was round and that Spain's national motto *Ne Plus Ultra* (Nothing Beyond) was wrong. As far back as Homer's time and beyond, people of the Mediterranean area believed that when one passed through the Strait of Gibraltar into the misty sea where the water-laden atmosphere of the Gulf Stream strikes the shores of northern Europe, he

53

entered "Hades," the abode of the dead. What faith it must have taken to sail through this gate into the wide ocean! How poor the world would be were there not great, adventurous souls who dare to out-believe the people of their time—of all time—and give to the world the new lands and things it so much needs.

Now sunny Italy spreads out before us. Mountains and valleys still surround us but on toward Rome the train speeds through more level land or perhaps it would be better described as less hilly. Vineyards and wineries come into view. Goats and cattle graze on the hillsides. Fruit trees with grapevines following wires stretched from tree to tree some ten to twenty feet above the ground appear on every side. Between the trees whose branches and vines are high enough to prevent interference with cultivation grow small fruits, vegetables and grain. People in America, where land is plentiful and the more easy and less intensified ways of cultivation are followed, have little idea of the burdens the people of overpopulated lands put themselves to in order to get enough from the soil to live by.

As the train sped Rome-ward, a young Irishman entered my compartment. He was on his way to the Vatican State to make observations regarding the faith that dominates his land. Soon another, an Italian, came. He knew a few English words that he picked up while stationed in northern Italy during his term of service in the army. I will always remember his kindness and eagerness to make the trip entertaining by pointing out places of interest along the way.

The old aqueducts that brought water to the homes and shops and baths of Rome in Caesar's day, which people cross continents and oceans to see, were as common to him as the barbwire that stretches along our highways is to us. The old castles that crown the mountain peaks, the monasteries, the convents that dot the hillsides and villages, the church spires that rise cloudward, were all familiar to him. His English vocabulary was small but he was an interesting travel mate. Our knowledge of the Italian was nil. But there is a language without words. It consists of sounds and groans, facial expressions, and motions that carry one through when words fail. Is not that what the wise man had in mind when he said, "A naughty person, a wicked man, . . . winketh with his eyes, he speaketh with his feet, he teacheth with his fingers" (Prov. 6:12, 13). This mode of communication can also be put to loftier purpose and better use and often is.

Finally, the glistening domes and spires of the Holy City, as it is sometimes called, came into view. But our journey was not yet ended. After a half hour's rest from his tiresome trip across the Alps and Apennines our electric motor was ready for the trip to Naples. As we approached our destination the friendly finger of our Italian friend pointed across the rocky hills and said, "Puteoli." Somehow this was a familiar sound and finally it began to dawn upon me that this is the city where Paul landed when he was taken to Rome upon the appeal of his case to Caesar.

NAPLES

Naples is badly battered as a result of the allied invasion. War is the same everywhere. Wherever and whenever the "horsemen of the Apocalypse" ride, the results are always the same. Hunger, disease, and death inevitably follow. The Relief Unit of the Mennonite Central Committee which was set up to supply food, clothing and shelter during and after the war is located on the third floor of a comfortable building, high above the traffic and commotion of the streets and thoroughfares of the city.

Sunday morning came and brought with it a bright sunny day. During the previous evening a jeepload of vacationers arrived from the MCC center of North Germany. The beautiful balconies afford one a splendid view of all the activities of a Sabbath morn in an Italian city. Church bells tolled on every side. Somberly dressed women, with heads veiled, prayer book and rosary in hand, hastened on to their places of worship for early mass. People came out of the dark, dismal, sunless recesses on the ground floor, which to them is home, some to lounge in the morning sun, others to wend their way to places of employment, or to the market in quest of food for the day. Street vendors began to appear, hawking their wares as they went and prospective buyers—mostly women—appeared on the balconies adjoining their apartments high above the streets, and from their lofty positions began bargaining with these loquacious hucksters. When the transaction was completed a basket containing the proper amount of money was let down by a rope and the purchase was delivered by the same means.

The war has done terrible things to the people of Italy as it has to people everywhere. Every land has always had its poor. This country has had its share, yea, and more! But since the war has wrecked so many homes, destitution is greater than ever and anything that gives promise of even meager shelter is occupied.

Our Sunday morning worship was held in the comfortable, airy living room of the Mennonite Central Committee center where Velma Schlabaugh was in charge and at this time she was alone. Later we attended the services of the Waldensian Church located in the midst of this large city. Here we found a house packed with people who came to listen to the Gospel as it is presented by Evangelical Christians. This group had its origin in the late twelfth century when the fires of the Inquisition were hot. These followers of Peter Waldo have always been intensely missionary minded and are now the most successful evangelistic group in Italy where they work among their own countrymen with a good deal of success.

POMPEII

One day there was the trip to Pompeii, a city of ruins. Here, in a short time, during the first Christian century, a whole area of life and culture was destroyed when the ashes fell. Pliny speaks of hearing rumblings and noises from the direction of Mt.

Vesuvius and of the sudden rise of a pillar of smoke that ascended skyward and assumed the shape of a pine tree—an Italian pine with a spreading mushroom head—which hung over the mountain for some time. Then this monster seemed to open wide its mouth and began to spew fire and ashes that engulfed three cities and, except for such as had fled, all were destroyed and buried.

Recently excavators have uncovered, at least in part, the ruins. Some of the homes remain as they were when they were overtaken. Housewives or servants that had bread ready for baking fled leaving their molded dough in the pans ready for the oven. Now, after almost nineteen centuries, this bread, turned into charcoal, still remains on the stove as it was when the disaster occurred. Chests in bankers' homes were found standing as they did when business was in progress. These and other remnants are evidences of the swiftness with which the destruction occurred.

Among these ruins one finds many evidences of a high culture. The bath—a large room decorated on sides and ceiling with paintings and murals—is quite intact and stands much as it did before the catastrophe. Paintings and decorations on the walls of homes where they were sheltered and protected are well preserved. The great amphitheater, with its ample stage and multiple entrances and exits, is an index of what Pompeian life must have been when it was at its heights. The beautiful courts where once fountains flowed and the fine marble statuary and carvings are among the tokens of a highly developed and extravagant social life. In the remnants of this culture one finds much that was beautiful and was to be desired. But life in those days also had its seamy side. In a small cell is what remains of one who was awaiting the executioner. In what was perhaps the section where denizens of evil plied their profession, are engravings, carvings, and statuary that indicate a depth of degradation that one can hardly conceive.

A return to Naples for dinner at 9:00 P.M., the hour when the Latins dine, brought us to a Chinese restaurant. Then a trip through the streets in a one-horse carriage with a high-hatted driver sitting on an elevated seat ahead of us helped us to visualize the goings on on the streets of an Italian city after darkness has fallen.

PUTEOLI

But Puteoli, the place where St. Paul first set his feet on Italy's shore, was near by and was calling. It is located about eight or ten miles from Naples in a pocket between the hills, facing the sea. The presence of a jeep with a group of Americans was the signal for the gathering of a crowd. But here in this city where church spires reach upward on every side no one seemed to know about Paul—no one except a Catholic priest. He spoke about him with a familiarity that made one feel that he had been on speaking terms with him. "If the city was then as it is now," he said, "this is the only place where he could have landed." What an experience just to have stood where perhaps he once stood or to have walked where he had walked!

THE APPIAN WAY

The trip from Naples to Rome took us over the Appian Way. Here on this great military highway the Roman legions once marched with their ensigns held high and their helmets and spears gleaming in the sun. Over this road, too, captives from other lands, many highly cultured, some royal children from the courts of kings, traveled in chains to march in the triumphal processions in the Imperial City where they were displayed as trophies of victory and destined to spend the rest of their days in slavery. This is a section of the country that one approaches almost with reverence because of its association with sacred memories. Along this road is where Paul and his associates traveled en route to Caesar's court where he as a Roman citizen hoped for a just adjudication of the charges against him. What emotions must have stirred his breast when the brethren met him at Appii forum and the Three Taverns and when the domes and spires of the city he had long desired to visit came into view! Here along the highway historians tell us the roadside was once lined for many miles with the bodies of crucified saints in the days of the Roman persecutions. What a ghastly sight this must have been with a cross bearing a dead or dying body every quarter of a mile or so.

Italy's countryside is beautiful after its own way. The stone buildings of the villages, monasteries, and convents blend so completely with the rocks that cover the hillsides that they are sometimes almost indiscernible. Farming is carried on as it is in most European countries. Oxen are widely used although modern machinery is also in evidence on the larger estates and farmsteads.

Traveling up the Appian Way led us through some beautiful country. The trip was made in a jeep drawn from the MCC collection in North Germany. Besides the four passengers it carried gasoline containers, baggage, a repair kit, spare tires, etc., all of which it behooves tourists to carry with them when they travel. Three passengers filled the capacity of the front seat. The rear was loaded with traveling paraphernalia and provided just sufficient room for one person. To occupy this place involved an acrobatic stunt of practically the first order. If the candidate was able to hit the vacant spot with his anatomy unscarred, he was lucky and was securely settled for most emergencies. The homemade top of steel with only a small glass on each side gave one the feeling of being confined to a cell.

Seeing Rome

By evening the towers and high places of Rome again came into view and our group was ready for a good meal and to enjoy the comfortable beds at a good hotel. Next day was a day of sight-seeing in this ancient stronghold of which Augustus boasted that he had found made of brick and left a city of marble. Voices of the past seemed to speak out of the old amphitheaters where the crowds were once entertained by saints fighting with the beasts. The old baths remain—some of them in ruins. In spite of the fact that the Romans are said to have once been experts in bathing there were some parts of this great city that looked as though the art needed some rejuvenating.

One does not get far with the tourists' guides until he realizes that the old churches and the auxiliary buildings and the art connected with them are the most important things in Rome aside from the old ruins. A person cannot help but notice also that the royalty which is so honored in lands where it still exists, here lives in the shadow of ecclesiastical dignity and glory.

The first tour took us through the city, past places of interest, to the Vatican. What a world of treasure one finds here! Mummies from the pyramids of Egypt, treasure from Babylon and Ur and Nineveh and Damascus to say nothing about the statuary and relics from Greece and other lands! One is awed by the paintings executed on the walls and ceilings by Michelangelo and many of the other great masters of art throughout the centuries. Here, too, is the Vatican Library where one of the oldest Greek manuscripts of the Bible is kept along with priceless papyri from the ash heaps of the Nile, parchment from Palestine and the ancient clay tablets from Medo-Persia, Babylonia and all the centers of culture of the Ancient East.

During the afternoon the party was taken to other scenes within and without the city. The first stop was at the Church of St. Peter in Chains in which is the great statue of Moses, a work of sculpture by Michelangelo. This was originally made, so the guide said, for St. Peters near the Vatican but because of some lack of agreement it found its way to the place where it now rests. The friar, who is in charge of the church and whose meditations were evidently interrupted by this troupe of chattering American tourists, was not in good humor and was not pleased with the disturbance. The great statue hewn out of a block of black granite represents the great lawgiver in all his virility and

60

strength which is so realistically portrayed that when the sculptor had completed his work and stood admiring it, it is said that he tapped the knee of the image with his hammer and asked, "Why don't you speak?"

From here the trip continued through the Gate of the Appian Way in the old wall of Rome. Here is where Paul entered the city. Beyond is the church of Quo Vadis. Tradition has it that when the persecution of the saints was at its heights in the Imperial City, St. Peter decided to abandon the place and was on his way out. On the spot where this chapel now stands, Christ is said to have met him and in answer to Peter's inquiry: "Quo Vadis" (whither are you going?) he received the reply: "I am going to Rome to be crucified again." Upon this, the fleeing apostle returned to his duties and when later he was sentenced to die, he chose to be crucified with his head downward.

The catacombs are subterranean passages and tunnels in which the Christians buried their dead in order to prevent the desecration of their cemeteries by the pagans. These great burial places are described by writers as cities underground. Once a person is underneath the surface, he realizes how enormous are these abodes of the dead. Passageways branch off from the main streets, and still others branch off from these side streets in many directions. Along the sides alcoves were dug out of the walls often two and three layers in height in which the bodies of the dead were deposited and the openings sealed with brick or stone. Many of these graves still bear the names of the occupants and often an epitaph which gives one a clue to the faith and hopes of those that were left behind to continue the struggle for life in a world where they were not wanted. Here and there, where the passageways crossed, were large open spaces somewhat like public squares, where Christians met for worship during the persecution of Decius and Diocletian. The catacombs of San Sebastian's gate are included in the American Express Company's tours. This place seemed to be in charge of the church.

61

English-speaking priests conducted the underground trip. One gets the feeling that the whole affair is highly commercialized and is now interpreted from the present-day traditions and viewpoint of the Church of Rome. As one wanders through the passageways and reads the inscriptions, sees the paintings, and the places of worship, he is made to realize what it cost the early Christians to maintain their faith.

But travelers cannot leave Rome without seeing St. Peter's, the glory of Rome and the pride of the Vatican. Here are gathered the remains of the popes. Many "relics" and scraps of bones of many of the "Saints" also repose in this place. Here, too, one sees an array of statuary and paintings and other works of art that came from the hands of the great masters who gave of their best to adorn and beautify this great cathedral. One sees many little chapels in the alcoves along the walls, also an elevated pulpit which they say is seldom used, and one notices the absence of any provision for the seating of crowds that pass through the building in which there is no arrangement for public worship. Underneath the shrines and statuary are basins of water and other provisions whereby worshipers may express their devotions. The toe of the black statue of St. Peter stands in need of replacement. It has not been able to withstand the impact of the ardent and multitudinous expressions of his devotees who pause to bestow upon it the prescribed token of their affection and respect.

The treasury where the vestments of deceased popes and other dignitaries are kept along with other treasures, rival—possibly exceed—the costly jewels and other valuables of British royalty which one finds in London Tower.

One comes away from such a place with mingled feelings. If the gathering of such a display of wealth, or the erection of such an ornate and indescribably beautiful building, is an acceptable expression of one's loyalty and devotion then this should be completely satisfying. When, however, one sees the ragged beggars, even some ribald friars, and other evidences of the ineffectiveness of such a mode of worship, his mind wanders to the simpler places that are adorned not with jewels or statuary or paintings or other material things but with lives renewed by faith in Christ their Redeemer and with humble spirits who serve human need.

FLORENCE AND MILAN

A person could easily spend days at Florence, once the home of the proud Medici, Dante, Petrarch, Galileo, Michelangelo and others of the long list of artists, sculptors, writers and popes. Milan, too, with its great cathedral, which rivals St. Peter's in Rome and St. Paul's in London, bids one stay and admire its beauty and browse around in its great libraries in Brera Palace and the Ambrosian College. But time had its limits and we hastened on to Venice, the city of canals and gondolas, built upon the waters.

VENICE

This is one of the ports from which ships sail to the orient. One evening after an interesting day in the mountains of Switzerland and northern Italy, we found ourselves on the boardwalks of this unique city that sits on stilts. An American Express Company agent turned us over to a trustworthy porter after having specified definitely the amount he was to receive for his service. We were led to one of the main waterways—the Grand Canal—and were soon on board a steamer which answered the purpose of a crowded streetcar in the cities you and I know. The hotel was comfortable and the food was good. We were in the heart of Venice not far removed from St. Mark's Cathedral, St. Mark's Square, Doges Palace, prisons and the Bridge of Sighs. It is evening, but the poet says:

> —it is not dark
> Within thy spacious place, St. Mark!
> The lights within, the lights without,
> Shine above the revel rout.

*   *   *

Facing the palace wherein doth lodge
The ocean-city's dreaded Doge
The palace is proud—but near it lies,
Divided by the "Bridge of Sighs,"
The dreary dwelling where the state
Enchains the captives of their hate;
These—they perish or they pine;
But which their doom may none divine;
Many have passed that Arch of Pain,
But none retraced their steps again.

What an interesting place this old city is! One hears no
clanging trolley cars, no honking automobiles and sees no donkey
carts. The only conveyance is by waterways, or on foot. Narrow
streets with little shops on each side offer everything from coca
cola to whatever one ordinarily buys in cities and towns.

A gondola trip took us up the Grand Canal which is to
Venice what Michigan Avenue is to Chicago. Here again it was
the old things—churches, monasteries, palaces, etc.,—that were
most important. En route we passed the place where Wordsworth spent his last days. The guide pointed out the famous old
palace with its lovely gardens where Barbara Hutton and her
Prince Charming lived during the first of her several honey-
moons. Along the way was the place where Browning, one of
England's famous poets, lived and died. Keats and Shelley died
in Rome.

But St. Mark's Piazza with its pigeons, children, and artists
has also an abundance of curbstone merchants who seek to direct
tourists to their places of business. If they happen upon one who
has American dollars they are quite as happy to exchange Italian
lire for them as they are to make a sale. The first day was spent
in exploring the city. Long walks from place to place on the
narrow streets led me to a glass factory whose product is famous
the world over. Here boys and girls with skillful hands turned
strands of glass into beads, brooches, and all kinds of ornaments
and animal figures. It was especially interesting to see them turn

the slender threads into Venetian dogs with long legs, long bodies, long noses, and queer tails. Italians seem to like dogs that way—the tails. I myself could never conceive of any plight in dogdom more pathetic than that of one trying to express his happiness with nothing to wag but a stub the size of an amputated thumb.

On the second morning an American showed up at the breakfast table. He was connected with some relief organization in Vienna and seemed to know his way around in the city. We decided that this would be a good time to do some shopping in Venetian specialties to take home with us. Being very unskilled at bargaining with shopkeepers, I readily consented that my companion should assume that part of our undertaking.

While going in and out of the narrow streets, past shops galore, we happened upon one with strands of beads beautifully strung, hanging by the doorside. The proprietors of the place were Jewish, some of the children of Abraham, who had found their way to this city as they do to all centers of population where there are wares to sell. They are remnants of a great race that through the centuries has suffered everything that people could suffer, but still they survive. Again and again they have risen out of the ashes of their misfortune and sorrow to pursue their divinely appointed course until they brought forth the world's greatest gift in Bethlehem's manger.

Neither of these people understood English or German so they called one who was evidently a daughter who spoke the latter language fluently. From the living quarters at the rear of the shop she came—this daughter of Rebecca—her features fair and eyes clear and tranquil as Solomon's Fish-pools in Heshbon. She is one of the thousands of millions that their brothers coveted for their sister Rebekah some four millenniums ago when she left her father's home in Haran to become the bride of Isaac and the mother of a people as numerous as the stars of the sky or the sands upon the shores of the sea. Her sisters sat in the markets of Babylon during the exile and in Damascus and Nineveh, in Egypt and Greece and Rome, as they do today in all the markets of the world where things are bartered or sold. Having selected each a strand of beads and a dog and a few other articles my friend unleashed his bargaining powers. When this offspring of Abraham's line sensed what seemed to her our penuriousness and our awkwardness and lack of skill in the art of bartering, the storm that lay beneath those serene features broke like one of those sudden squalls on Galilee and she proceeded to tell us what she thought of Americans with their pockets bulging with dollars. I think she actually spat as she turned on her heel and hied herself into the shop. As she went she turned her red head and said something over her shoulder that neither of us fully understood—maybe it was in Hebrew. It included some Biblical words.

With this incident, our shopping expedition collapsed, and I resolved once and for all that those glass dogs with their funny tails could hang by the doorside until they return to the sand from which they were taken and the beads could swing in the breeze until they molder into dust and blow into the sea, before I'll roil the fish-pools of Heshbon again.

When it rains in Venice drabness overwhelms one. The gaiety dies down and pedestrians walk under dripping umbrellas and slosh through the narrow wet streets. At the Piazza people huddle under the arcades. Pigeons retreat to their roosts on the facades of St. Mark's until the bells ring, then they dash forth like bats out of the darkness. At the edge of the sidewalk in a sheltered nook sits an artist with brush in hand reproducing St. Mark's on canvas with the motley forms of the passing stream of people reflected on the wet street. The winged lion on the pedestal high above the pavement seems to spread his wings more widely in protest against the weather as he guards the Ducal Palace against the winds and storms of the sea, while the gilded lion high in the clock tower scowls more bitterly at the dripping crowds below. What tag ends of tourists remain are hibernating in their hotels and "hide-outs" today, little seen and less heard —perhaps thinking of home. But the bronze men on top of the great clock tower are on duty as they have been every day for centuries. They, too, must have caught the spirit of their surroundings for they seem to wield their sledges more mightily as they strike the passing hours. It's raining in Venice—a city built on the sea.

> Oh, Venice! Venice! When thy marble walls
> Are level with the waters, there shall be
> A cry of nations o'er thy sunken halls,
> A loud lament along the sweeping sea!

VIII

TRAILWAYS
THROUGH GERMANY

Early one morning—too early to please the customs officials
—in late August a station wagon bearing a group of MCC
workers drove across the Rhine at Basel, Switzerland, into Germany. The party was scheduled to make its way through some of
the most scenic parts of the country which was once the home of
my ancestors. Consequently I looked forward to this trip with
much anticipation and deep interest. I recalled again incidents
my mother's father related about his childhood at Waldek near
Kassel where he played by the old mill. Stories of the loveliness
of the Pfalz (Palatinate) along the Rhine rose out of the past
and brought to memory again some of the folksongs and tales
we had listened to as children at our mother's knee.

Though it was early in the day the thrifty population was
astir and already at work. It was the time of the grain harvest.
The fields were teeming with reapers who wielded the scythe,
while others bound the sheaves as they did long ago before modern machinery made its advent. Now and then there were machines at work. Occasionally there was a mower drawn by
horses or oxen and less frequently a person saw a self-binder.
Instead of the large fields we are accustomed to, these crops
grow on narrow strips of land adjoining each other. The colors
of the grains, vegetables, and root crops adorn the landscape
with a charming beauty that makes the countryside look like
a little paradise.

The life of these rural communities apparently centers in the village, many of which are old and bear the mellowness of age and maturity. Here children play in the streets and in the evening the young folk gather to while away the hours in such pastimes as they know, and their elders enjoy themselves in conversation or perhaps sit quietly dreaming as older people do. How quiet and restful and how intriguing these places are! One would like to linger here for weeks and get a taste of the life as it is lived in seeming contentment. To them our isolated farm home would no doubt seem dull, and our rushing hither and yon would appear confusing and useless as much of it in reality is.

The road led through the famed Black Forests whose pines and evergreens cover the mountain slopes to their very peaks. Beautiful little lakes lie hidden deep within the valleys and now and then an ancient castle raises its hoary head high above its surroundings. During the day our trail led to one of these remnants of Germany's past, where once the proud Hohenzollerns lived secure within the lofty walls and battlements which still stand as they did of yore. From its towers one may gaze for miles across the smoky hills and valleys, and see in fancy the lords with their retainers, lances and armor gleaming, coming up the winding trails to the security of this vast establishment.

Today its life is stilled except for the rare festal occasions and other uses which are made of its facilities. When we crossed over its drawbridge and entered its wide portals we found some of its quarters occupied by a group of young theologues who, we were told, were holding a retreat here in the shadows of the past. They were led across the court by a Lutheran minister who greeted us reverently with a beautiful salutation: *"Crüss Gott."*

During the American invasion, we were informed, one of the Hohenzollern princesses—if they are still recognized as such —captivated the heart of one of the American army officers. Once more the old castle became alive. Here within the chapel the vows were spoken and in these vast rooms the festivities were held. Again the chandeliers were burnished and the lights glittered. The long tables were spread and the rooms reeked with the aroma of the field and forest—the stag and the roe. Once more the draperies of the bridal chamber were hung and lithe forms glided over the floor of the ball-room to the strains of music such as the great German masters composed. One can almost see the "misty" forms of the proud, bearded proprietors of the past arrayed against the wall in their princely regalia, gazing upon scenes that once charmed and delighted them. But when we saw the place the wedding celebration was over and the guests were gone. In some less pretentious quarters the princess sat waiting for her Romeo to return from his Texas oil fields while skeins of political "yarn" in whose entanglements she had become enmeshed, were being unwound.

Our route took us through the American Zone with its PXs (U.S. military stores) where gasoline, ice cream, candies and knickknacks, such as Americans buy, are sold. There, too, are lunch counters and restaurants serving food in American style. These are little islands of the U.S.A. in a sea of alien tradition that has its roots deep in the past. Here German girls, neatly attired, waited tables and took our order in terminology that we understood. When eggs were ordered they asked: "Straight up or over?" just as they do in the places where we eat at home.

The soil of Germany is historic ground. Incidents that were forgotten came alive again as familiar names appeared in their native setting. Somewhere in these parts Wallenstein sought to read his destiny in the stars while hostile armies flamed around him. To the east lies historic Weimar where Goethe and Schiller once lived and wrought and immortalized their names while bringing undying renown to their native land. There, too, lie the beautiful Harz Mountains, quiet and serene retreats, over whose hilltops the sage of Weimar looked when he scribbled on the wall of his lodge the words of the famed "Slumber Song of Summer":

Uber allen Gipfeln ist Ruh.
In allen Wipfeln spürest du
Kaum einen Hauch!

Within the bounds of this country lived also others who contributed to its wealth in the field of literature and music and art to say nothing of their achievements in science and other fields of knowledge. In the period along with Goethe belong the galaxy of "Nines"—Father Gleim, Lessing, Schubert, Schiller, Rückert, and Heine—all of whom made their advent into the world in years that ended with "nine." How poor the world would be if it should be deprived of the work of all these high bards along with that of a host of others who filled the ages with their melody and song!

Among these great were some of lesser renown who had no advantage of learning or training nor of birth or position, whose names are not found in halls of fame nor in the register of the elite. They came out of obscurity and sang their songs amid the cares of the common life with its toil and perplexities and then disappeared too often unhonored and unsung. Such an one was Johanna Ambrosius, a German housewife who toiled over the kitchen stove and washtub to provide for her children and her spouse. Only one like she could sing as she sang out of the experience of her careworn and tired soul:

Den lieben langen Tag
Vom frühen Morgen an
Freut' mich die Stude wo
Ich schlafen gehen kann.
Wenn sich die müde Seel'
Kraft suchet im Gebet
Dann fühl' ich, wie der Herr
An meinem Lager steht.

One would suspect from the following lines that there were times when she must have been keenly conscious of her lack of preparation. Her declensions, conjugations and syntax might not have passed the test of the schools of her day nor of ours

71

but she used what she knew—her dialect, her words, and her experiences with no thought of apology and perhaps no idea of winning acclaim from the circle of her admirers:

> Richtet nich nach Form and Rythem,
> Davon hab' ich nichts gelernt.
> Denkt, es sind bescheid'ne Blüten,
> Hie and da vom Tau besternt;
> Hie and da vom Storm zerbiessen,
> Wie sie bieten Feld und Flur,
> Meinem Herzen all' entrissen
> Gleich der Mutterbrust Natur.

What a ray of light must have come into this humble life when one day she was invited to come across the English Channel to be the guest of Britain's honored. Here she was given a taste of a side of life she had never known. She was presented to king and queen, to men and women of letters and people of high renown. The schools, to which she had been a stranger, did her homage. But she returned, unspoiled and contented, to her humble home and family. When she saw the shoreline of her native land rise out of the sea, words began to flow and she wrote:

> Ich lass von meiner Heimat nicht
> Was man auch sagen wollt,
> Sie hebt vor allen Landen sich
> Heraus wie echtes Gold.
> Lasz blüh'n das Glück aus anderwärts
> In reich'rer Farbenpracht
> Ich weisz wie in der Heimat mir
> Die Sonne nirgends lacht.
>
> Ich lass von meiner Heimat nicht,
> Sie birgst das Eltern haus,
> Vor diesem stillen Heiligtum
> Zieh' ich die Schuhe aus.
> Da ist ein jeder Ort geweiht,
> Nichts Heil'gres giebt's wie das,
> Da wird auch ohne Priesterwort
> Hein Aug' von selber nasz.

Translate these lines, you say? Forbid such travesty! The words of no language I know can convey the feeling and sentiment of this humble soul whose spirit rose and whose hope mounted when she looked ahead to the time when she would no longer be judged by the limits and meagerness of her earthly lot. Friends of mine have searched in vain the shelves of libraries and used-book stores on the continent for the treasures from the pen of this peasant woman and returned with empty hands. But from the secluded nooks in which they lie some passing travelers will draw the inspiration and comfort and above all the faith which they reflect:

> Heb' nur empor dein Auge,
> In Hoffnung und vertrau'n,
> Ist auch mein weg verborgen,
> Bald wirst das Glük du schau'n!
> Lasz deine Thränen rinnen
> Nur nieder in die Flut,
> Und denk' bei Kreuz und Leide:
> Dein Vater meint es gut!

Coming down the mountainside there lay before us a smiling sheet of water—Tittesee. Quaint little shops and homes lined the roadside that skirted the shores of the lake. Close by, the Black Forest clocks are made. From the markets along the way they are sold and along with beautiful wood carvings of all sorts they find their way into homes of travelers from afar.

From this restful, friendly little spot where one would like to remain indefinitely the road led through Tuebingen, an old University center and through Backnang near Stuttgart where there was located at that time a large refugee camp. Evening found our party at Heilbronn where the river Neckar flows. Here the Mennonite Central Committee has set up a Community Center equipped with sewing machines for the use of the women of the neighborhood. In it is included also a shoe repair shop, a recreation center, a reading room and a hall which is used for worship services. This is a little oasis of consolation and hope in a wilderness of desolation and destruction. About 7:30 on the evening of December 4, 1944, a fleet of American bombers dropped their entire load of phosphorescent bombs on this place. Within a few minutes the city became a burning inferno, and thousands were crippled, maimed, dead, or covered within the ruins. At the edge of a beautiful forest outside the city in what was once a field of grain, more than twenty thousand bodies lie uncoffined in unmarked graves where grass now grows and flowers bloom to hide the bitter scars of war. On the side facing the timber stands a large wooden cross as a symbol of faith in a Redeemer whose sacrifice holds forth the only hope of better things.

An evening trip to the farmsteads of the Felman Brothers gave us a glimpse of what intensive farming is like on the large estates. Here were barns filled with the choicest livestock—large work oxen, fine horses, and choice dairy cattle. From the fields, gardens, and orchards came a wide variety of grains, vegetables, fruits, and other products with which these thrifty and industrious people, together with a host of others, are helping to reduce Germany's want and lifting it out of its need and dependence upon the ministry of hands from across the sea for food to live by. Close by lie the shattered remains of what was once Loewenstein Castle, owned by a Loewenstein prince who sought security for his possessions in this retreat only to have it bombed out of existence. Only part of one wall remains.

In this section is located also the castle of "Weibertreu" fame. Tradition has it that long ago the inhabitants of this community were driven to the security of this fortress by hostile invaders by whose decree all the men were doomed to destruction. Through negotiations that followed it was agreed that the women should be released and were granted the right to take with them all of their possessions they could carry. When the terms of surrender had been fully confirmed and the gates were thrown open, the faithful wives emerged each carrying a man on her back. The old castle hung in the haze of an autumn morning when we saw it but one could easily imagine a long line of devoted women coming down the hill, wending their way along the crooked path, each carrying her precious burden.

Eastward from Heilbronn,

> In the valley of the Pegnitz,
>   Where across blue meadow-lands,
> Rise the blue Franconian Mountains,
>   Nüerenberg the ancient stands.
>
> Where when art was still religion,
>   With a simple, reverent heart,
> Lived and labored Albrecht Düer,
>   The evangelist of art.
>
> Through these streets so broad and stately,
>   These obscure and dismal lanes,
> Walked of yore the Meistersingers,
>   Chanting rude poetic strains.
>
> Here Hans Sachs, the cobbler poet,
>   Laureate of the gentler craft,
> Wisest of twelve Wise Masters,
>   In huge folios sang and laughed.
>
> Not thy councils, nor thy Kaisers,
>   Win for thee the world's regard,
> But thy painter, Albrecht Dürer,
>   And Hans Sachs, thy cobbler bard.
>   —LONGFELLOW

From Heilbronn, through Heidelberg, Mannheim, and Neustadt to Kaiserslautern we passed through forests that have long been the pride of Germany and an example to the world of what thrift and care can do in the way of conserving a nation's resources of timber. Under the generous care of the government, these wooded areas have been preserved, improved, and replenished. They furnish not only the lumber and fuel and wood for other needs but they provide also alluring playgrounds and pleasure resorts for the nature-loving population. When I passed through this section of the country the forests were in the hands of aliens embittered with their losses and sufferings. Large cut-over, denuded spaces on the mountainsides bore evidence of the ruthlessness with which they did their work. Sawmills lined the highways and trainload after trainload of lumber went across the border each week as reparations of war. What confusion and ruin such upheavals as those of the years 1938 to 1945 bring! When one looks upon the wreckage and wastage he wonders who could be proud of any part he may have had in bringing about such a spirit of vengeance and destruction of life and property.

A trip from Neustadt to Hamburg took us part of the way over the famed Autobahn which was built in Hitler's day and which was his pride and delight. Along the highway was the famous field from which the planes flew that shuttled in and out of Berlin during the winter months when the airlift kept the city supplied with food and coal. This road is one of the beautiful drives that takes one through a country of rolling hills—often mountains in the distance—where the wayside is bordered with fields that look like a garden.

To the East behind the "Iron Curtain," enshrouded in a pall of secrecy and mystery lies Leipzig, famed for its old University and its long list of great men. There, too, stands Halle with its University of Pietistic origin where Spener taught and wrote his *Pia Desideria* which infused warmth into the spiritual stirrings of his time. Along with him wrought August Francke, great pastor and professor in the university, and Benjamin Swartz who was one of the sixty missionaries which the Pietist schools of Halle sent to foreign lands. Out of this movement came great institutions for destitute children. Among these halls of learning was the Danish-Halle mission which has the honor of having produced the earliest Protestant foreign mission work. Out of its life and spirit came the Moravian Brotherhood, which touched

76

John Wesley. Through the great German Pietist minister, Raritan, Gilbert Tennent received his inspiration which set off the Great Awakening that rocked America and brought thousands into the fold of the Lord.

Within the haze of the Soviet orbit are the cities of Weimar and Jena, once stars of the first magnitude in Germany's firmament but now enshaded in clouds of delusion that hang over them like a deadly miasma. Wittenberg, also, where Tetzel's infamous sale of Indulgences brought to a climax Luther's ire, lies within this sector. Once the atmosphere rang with the hammer strokes of this young Augustinian monk when he nailed his ninety-five theses to the door of the parish church and showed his disdain for the Papal Bull of Excommunication by burning it publicly in the presence of a group of professors and students. That day the discontented masses who were seeking new light found their leader and Martin Luther became their hero. Summoned to Worms to give an account of his heretical notions, he entered the city on the morning of April 16, 1525, in a two-wheeled Saxon cart accompanied by a few companions. Two thousand people greeted him and conducted him to his lodgings. The following day he met the Diet composed of dignitaries of the church and state before whom he was to give an account of his writings and his conduct. The star of Luther perhaps never shone brighter than it did on that day when he calmly and with composure and dignity defended his cause and refused to retract one single statement unless it could be "proven by the Scripture or evident reason" that he was wrong, and concluded his address with the following dramatic statement: "Here I stand, I cannot do otherwise, God help me! Amen." Throwing up his arm in the gesture of a knight who had won the tournament he quietly slipped away from the hissing papists into the arms of his friends. Lutheranism was born and the battle was on!

High in the church tower at Münster in North Germany hang three iron cages in which three misguided leaders of a radical reform group were confined after their plan to bring in the kingdom of God by force, had failed. Through the centuries from 1536 their bones lay bleaching in the wind and sun until 1870 when they were finally removed to a less conspicuous place. But the cages still hang as a memorial of what was then and is now—by some people—considered an act of piety. In the private dining room of a restaurant near the scene of this tragedy hang miniature replicas of these cages with the following quotation inscribed upon the walls:

Jan von Leyden, Kipperdolhnck un Kraeching sind fangen,
Daud Makte un on Lamboetilaon hangen.

Some miles from the city of Hamburg by a large Lynden tree stands a little white house known as "Menno Lynde" which it is claimed sheltered Menno Simons when he was forced to flee from his native Holland as a result of his Anabaptist activities. Here, it is said, he established his home and set up his print shop in the attic from whence books and tracts began to flow. A little distance farther on in a field of grain stands a stone which marks what is thought to be his last resting place. Grateful refugees from other lands have cleaned the enclosure within the iron fence where his body lies and have adorned the place with flowering plants and shrubs as a token of the love they bear the founder of the faith that is so precious to them.

At Gronau, near the German-Holland border, is a large refugee camp where homeless people who have wandered into the country are gathered and maintained while waiting for the way to clear for them to migrate to the New World. This camp is maintained by the Mennonite Central Committee. A large building, which was before the war a private home, is used for living quarters for the employees and as office space for the large staff of clerks, stenographers, counselors and statisticians who are employed here. Across the street stands a spacious dwelling house which has now been converted into a hospital of some sixty-bed capacity staffed with competent medical men and

78

trained nurses. Here the ailments of the camp are taken care of. In a grove of beautiful shade trees are located the buildings formerly used as a social center by the local Mennonites. In these quarters the refugees are housed and fed. As one wandered through the crowded halls he was led to wonder how people can continue to exist amid such congestion. A person comes away from places such as this with a feeling of deep gratitude for the spirit of the noble company of men and women who are devoting their life and energy to the need of these unfortunate, homeless, unwanted folks.

When I returned to Germany for the meeting of the MCC workers at Neustadt it was past the middle of September. The trip took us through the beautiful Pfalz (Palatinate) in the Rhineland. The gathering of grapes was in full swing. Everywhere one saw wagons loaded with large tubs, drawn by slow moving oxen. On these were gathered the juicy clusters for the wineries. The leaves were beginning to turn and the smells of autumn were in the air. It was wonderful to drive over the hills of a country so beautiful, where the kind, thrifty, patient village people were deeply absorbed with the duties which harvest brings. Here and there were demolished bunkers of the Siegfried Line and now and then a village that did not escape the eye of those who sought to break the morale of the people by bringing destruction to their very doors.

A meeting of the personnel of the Mennonite Central Committee was to take place at Neustadt the middle of September 1949. It was held in what was before the war a social center for officers of the German army. Near by was a hostel built for the Hitler youth, with comfortable sleeping quarters and dining room facilities where those who were in attendance on this occasion found shelter and care. These were glorious days filled with inspiration as we mingled with these young people full of the strength and the enthusiasm of their youth. In this instance it was all the more so because here their powers and abilities were consecrated to helpful and serious purposes. They were strangers from the western world who had come to help mollify the wounds of war and bring again hope to a people whose world had crumpled at their feet. What a task to devote one's life to! And how appropriate it is for Christians to dedicate themselves to causes such as these young men and women serve.

Sunday morning found a busload of us at Kohlhof for worship with the Mennonite congregation. The afternoon was spent at Speyer, the scene of Reformation Diets and disputations where now stands the great Kaiser Wilhelm "Gädechtnis Kirche," dedicated to the memory of Martin Luther and paid for with contributions which came from many lands. Here, as elsewhere, it is the old things—old churches, old, old castles, old paintings and tombs—that are most highly esteemed. Each Sunday groups of people from many places come to see these famous remnants of the past. Besides seeing places of interest, we met lovely people in their native haunts who live their simple everyday lives doing the things upon which the world is so dependent for its existence. What a tragedy that every so often a people so kind, in whom resides so much that is good and lovely, must suffer as these have suffered because of misguided leadership and the unsanctified designs of some of its neighbors!

When a person sees the destruction and waste of war, the ruined cities, men and women maimed in body and soul, unwanted little ones imposed upon unwilling victims, often through the lust of a victorious soldiery, the situation looks despairing. But when on the other hand he sees the thrifty, industrious and intelligent peasantry working, and the earnest effort of the nation's leaders in planning for the restoration of the ruins of their homeland, his faith rises again. Surely a people in whom there is so much good will not cease to exist and if given time they will again lift their nation out of its ashes and restore it to its place in the sun.

IX

ALONG THE DIKES
AND CANALS OF HOLLAND

Netherlands is a land of tulips and flowers, thrifty people and a lore of history with which Dutch Anabaptism is closely connected. When I crossed the border one morning in late August the tulips had long since shed their blooms but other flowers had taken their place and filled the atmosphere with fragrance and the countryside with color. The skies were blue and the sun gave off a kindly warmth which afforded us days of comfort and enjoyment. Windmills flopped their wings lazily in the breeze as if in protest against the drudgery of lifting the water over the dikes and pouring it into the sea.

I was on the way to Amsterdam where the Mennonite Central Committee has the headquarters from which it directed its relief work during the days of Holland's need following the war. Naturally the landscape is almost monotonously flat. Much of it has been reclaimed from the sea and consequently is below sea level. This, however, is relieved by the beauty of the lakes and dikes and canals that are seen everywhere. Roads often follow these waterways and not infrequently they are on top of the ditch banks. Clumps of timber, farmsteads, fields of growing grain and meadowland filled with herds of the famed Friesian dairy cattle make one forget the contour of the country which might otherwise seem as drab and uninteresting as are the level, treeless plains of the United States and Canada.

This process of reclamation has been going on for a long time. Dutch engineers are past masters at dike building. For centuries they have been throwing up their embankments to set new boundaries for the sea. Previous to the war several new tracts had been reclaimed and were brought into production. Then hostile armies cut the banks and flooded the land with the salt-laden waters. New buildings that had sheltered families who were happy in the pursuit of their labors, were reduced to ruins, and the occupants were compelled to give way before the encroaching floods and see their homes destroyed.

More than a century ago, I was told, a Mennonite engineer draughted the plans for a dike across the mouth of the Zuider Zee which indents the northern part of Holland. In recent years this project was undertaken and previous to the last world war it was finished. Since then the water is being gradually drained off and by the middle of this decade (ca. 1955) it is hoped to have the major part of it completed. Then will come the dike builders and canal diggers who will empty the small pockets of water that remain or confine them within safe bounds as lakes and resorts that will become recreation spots. The floor of what was once the sea will then furnish homes, farmsteads and village sites for many of the thrifty folk of the nation.

Racially the Dutch are of Teutonic origin. Historians tell us that the majority of them are of the old Bavarian stock. This element is said to comprise about seventy per cent of the population. The rest is made up of Flemish and Friesians. They are a peace-loving race, thrifty, industrious, and progressive. During the first World War, they together with several other small nations of Europe, maintained their neutrality though surrounded by hostile armies on every side. During the second World War that same situation would likely have prevailed had not the country been ruthlessly invaded. We think of them as a stable, conservative people who love their homes, their homeland and their families.

But at the time when the rulers of other lands were adding new territory to their domains, these people sought also to expand their holdings. By some means they acquired New Amsterdam—now New York—and some islands of the sea. Emigrants from Holland settled in South Africa and set up what gave promise of becoming an independent empire in the southern part of that continent only to lose it to the British at the turn of the last century.

Judging from some of the legends and tales of the past their sailors had their hands also in the mischief that the sea rovers made among the treasure-laden vessels that were sailing homeward with loot and booty taken from the people of the New World that had just been discovered.

> Simon Danz has come home again
> From cruising about with his buccaneers.
> He has singed the beard of the King of Spain,
> And carried away the Dean of Jaen
> And sold him in Algiers.
>
> Restless at times with heavy strides,
> He paces his parlor to and fro;
> He is like a ship that at anchor rides
> And swings with the rising and falling tides
> And tugs at her anchor tow.
>
> So he thinks he shall take to the sea again,
> For one more cruise with his buccaneers,
> To singe the beard of the King of Spain,
> And capture another Dean of Jaen,
> And sell him in Algiers.

Thus far Holland's kings have escaped with their beards unsinged and its queen still carries her head on her shoulders. It is one of the few monarchies that survived the upheaval of the last quarter century. Its queen is greatly loved and is, no doubt, worthy of all the affection and honor her people bestow upon her. The Royal Palace is outside The Hague, its capital city. It is a long sprawling building set in the midst of spacious grounds which are beautifully landscaped. Compared with the ornate and extravagant domiciles of the royalty of other lands, this place is quite modest, and if one may judge from its exterior, it fittingly symbolizes the nation's sturdiness, frugality and thrift —virtues that have become strangers in many lands.

In Holland there is complete religious liberty. The Reformed Church claims the largest membership. The rest of the church-going population belong to the Roman Catholic, the Old Catholic, the Jews, and smaller Protestant or evangelical sects. Among the latter is the Anabaptist or Mennonite group which numbers around fifty thousand members. Though this body is small it occupies a position of influence in the country that is altogether out of proportion to its size. These people figure large in the fields of industry and the learned professions such as law, medicine, and teaching as well as in the arts and crafts. Among them have been several artists of note whose paintings hang in the galleries of the state and of other lands. Many have occupied high and important positions in the affairs of the nation. Their names are familiar in the fields of jurisprudence—some having held positions in the Supreme Court. Others were active in statescraft and have served their country in its legislative bodies and in the higher councils of the government. Though many of them are occupied in learned professions, the majority remain "children of the soil"—farmers and husbandmen—humble, industrious, highly skilled tillers of the land as are their coreligionists wherever they are found.

Amsterdam escaped the destruction and ravages of the war. Judging from the present condition of its buildings the damage was small. Other cities like Rotterdam which were industrial and shipping centers suffered devastation that beggars description. But the Dutch with their characteristic zeal and energy have already pulled themselves out of the ruins and are on the road to recovery. New buildings are rearing their heads above the rubble. Harbors are being cleared of the debris and wreckage of war. Docks are being repaired or rebuilt and put into service.

A Netherlands country scene.

Church where Menno Simons first preached, Pingjum, Holland.

Monument to Menno Simons, Holland.

A German village.

Vineyards on the hillsides in the Palatinate.

Churches dot the landscape in Alsatian land.

The author beside Menno Simons monument, Germany.

Swiss children of the mountains. Jungfrau in the background.

Grape harvest in Switzerland.

The Grossmunster Church at Zürich where Manz and Grebel held their famed disputations.

Its freighters and passenger ships again sail the seas and shuttle back and forth between many parts of the world. The scars on her landscape will gradually be eradicated but the bruises of the soul heal slowly unless mollified by grace divine. Memories of their experience during the war are bitter!

A trip through the city took us to the Seminary of the Dutch Mennonites. The school was not in session but the library was open. Through the courtesy of the custodian we were shown this remarkable and most valuable collection of Anabaptist materials in the world. Judging from the names that are carved in the tables around which the prospective theologians and scholars sit, the students who study here have at least some characteristics in common with those one meets with on the campuses of American Colleges and Universities.

A Sunday morning worship service at the Singel Doopsgesinde Church was not only interesting but edifying. After the preliminary service, which consisted of singing, Scripture reading, comments and prayer, the sermon was delivered by a woman ordained to the ministry. As I think of it now, her address was the most finished piece of pulpit oratory I have ever heard. Not only was it well composed and excellently delivered but its content was Biblical and its exposition sound. One came away knowing what was wrong with the rich man who had to enlarge his barns in order to provide storage for his crops. The church is an old one, hidden from the main thoroughfare by other buildings which were placed between it and the passing public in order to screen it from critical and unfriendly eyes in the days when worship such as was conducted here was not tolerated.

But this game of persecuting those who were not in accord with the prevailing and dominant practices of the church that was in power was one at which both sides could play. Not only did those of the Protestant faith go into hiding when the Catholics were in control but when it happened as it sometimes did that the authority shifted, then the Catholics had to find secret

85

shelters for their meetings. One of these places is known as the "Church of the Blessed Christ in the Attic." It was pointed out to us in a thickly populated section of Amsterdam. High above the pavement in the secluded top story of a building the worshipers used to gather for their services. Today the windows are boarded up and the space where masses were said and confessions were heard is now used for other more secular purposes. Such remnants of the misguided zeal of earlier followers of Christ belong to bygone days in countries like Holland where worshipers now have the freedom to follow their conviction as long as they are decent. In some of the other lands where Christianity failed so miserably because of the poor way in which it was represented and practiced, the liberty that once existed is now eclipsed and darkness reigns again. What a tragedy!

A day in the city and its environs under the guidance of Dr. Hylkema, a devoted Christian and a good companion, took us along the dikes and canals to such places as Zaandam where children played in the street and housewives gathered around the hucksters that sold their wares from a truck or other conveyance. Here we visited an old Mennonite church with its elevated pulpit and sand-covered floor. In the rear was a room, now used for storage, in which a fireplace covered with porcelain tile was decorated with pictures illustrating Bible characters or bits of Biblical history. This was one of the devices, so our guide said, by which children were taught the Scripture on long winter evenings when the family gathered around the glowing embers by the hearthside. A kindly old woman whose husband is the keeper of this church admitted us to the building. When we stopped at the home of this good soul to return the key and express our appreciation for her kindness we were invited to stay for tea. She sat in her quiet room loaded with the perfume of flowers. Her kindness and calmness took me back in thought to a place I often visited in my childhood—grandmother's house.

The rich fragrance of her plants and the enticing aromas of her kitchen are inseparably connected with the thoughts and memories of her name. The glory and goodness of those quiet, leisurely days have long since been lost and we are now so loaded with conveniences and labor-saving devices that we can hardly pause in the multitude of duties to be neighborly. And yet we talk about imposing our "American way of life" upon those who have time to be "rich in the spirit" and are contented with the simple things they can have.

Our trip also led us out to the island of Maarken, off the west coast of the Zuider Zee. Here the village folk dressed in their quaint garb of long ago spend their time fishing and selling novelties—wooden shoes, post cards and knickknacks—to tourists and sight-seers. When this body of water is drained and turned over to farmers and husbandmen, the fisher folk and vendors of curios and novelties will need to look elsewhere for fishing grounds and customers for their foods drawn from the deep.

One day, in company with a couple from Heerewegen, Jan and Mary (Berkman) Matthijssen, and a relief worker from the U.S.A., we drove a requisitioned Ford to Friesland—the Menno Simons country—in northern Holland. En route we saw the devastation which the floods had wrought when the dikes were cut during the war. Lands had become marshes again and buildings were filled with the sand and silt of the sea. But the patient farmer folk, children of the good earth, refused to be defeated. Already some of the fields have been reclaimed and are on the way to become productive again.

Our route took us across the twelve-mile-long dike which cuts off the Zuider Zee from the North Sea. The top of this wall has become a beautiful drive with towers of observation along the way. During the war the German armies set up all kinds of barricades across this causeway which connects the north country in order to retain their control over the area. Some of them still remain.

This section is rich in Mennonite lore. Somewhere here Menno Simons was born and began his ministry as a priest in the Church of Rome. The building in which it is thought that he held mass and heard confessions still stands at Witmarsum. Another small church at Pingjum, now "hidden" from the street by a little store and dwelling house, is at present used by the Mennonites for their services. This place may also have been in use in Menno's day and it is possible that he proclaimed the Gospel from its pulpit. Outside of Witmarsum, a little distance off the road, stands a stone shaft erected to his memory. Here, too, he did a large part of his work in the interest of bringing together the Anabaptist groups and molding them into a united body of believers. This monument marks the place on which it is thought the building stood in which he ministered after he left the Roman Church.

Heerewegen, or literally, "The ways of the Lord" which was previously a place frequented by the aristocracy, was used as a home for children in the days following the war when the Mennonite Central Committee maintained feeding stations throughout a number of European countries as well as homes to shelter the homeless little ones that were adrift. More recently it has been set apart under MCC management as a place for conferences and meetings of various kinds such as fall within the scope of the purpose of this organization.

The buildings consist of a large house for the manager and guests, rooms for conferences, devotions, and prayer meetings. A lovely Swiss cottage bearing the inscription *"Freuen Morgen, Keine Sorgen, Gott Lob!"* houses the Library and Offices of the Dutch Peace group. From its motto it derives its name: *"Gott Lob."* The "Hans-und-Gretel" cottage shelters the male personnel and a larger structure which once served as a coach house has been remodeled and transformed into a chapel-hostel known as the Menno meetinghouse. These buildings are located on a twenty-acre wooded tract, with paths and quiet nooks for rest and meditation. It is what its present usage suggests, "House of Peace." After the busy weeks preceding my arrival in the Netherlands the quietness of Heerewegen was a resting place indeed. At that time the children's work was being discontinued. And the change as above described was in the process of being carried through.

One Sunday morning we drove from this quiet, secluded spot to Amsterdam. It seemed as though the whole population was out on bicycles or in motor boats. In my travels I have become accustomed to seeing new things and am not too much surprised when something unusual appears. But this seemingly endless, colorful array of people, young and old, holiday bent, was so different that it became impressive. What a stream of happy folk this was, moving along on wheels! It was far more charming and intriguing than any automobile procession with its blaring horns, screeching brakes and noisome smells of gasoline, loaded with folks whose nerves in such a congestion are tense, their faces hard, their dispositions irritable, and their tempers short.

In Holland people are never far removed from water. The canals, lakes and the sea furnish opportunity for boating. Recreation centers of all sorts spring up along these waterways and lakesides. Around some of them have grown up camps for the youths of religious groups. In ventures such as this the Holland Doopsgesinden have made much progress. Here people young and old come for rest and recreation as well as for religious retreats and meetings of various kinds.

Mennonite Central Committee centers on the continent are cosmopolitan places. Workers from all branches of the Mennonite Church, gathered from many states of the Union and provinces of Canada, come together here. Some are connected with the staff. Others come and go. Beside these there are some European nationals connected with the organization who are serving with their kinsmen in the faith as they minister to the physical and spiritual needs of the people "In the Name of Christ." How widely the centuries had separated us! Miles that stretch from the steppes of Russia, yea, from far Siberia to the shores of the United States and Canada lay between us who had a common origin and a common fatherland only a few centuries ago. But even more widely, it seems, had we become separated spiritually until we were virtually strangers to each other. Then came two globe-girdling wars that brought us together again in the fellowship of a ministry to the suffering and needy. There, at those altars where we served with each other, we learned anew how much we still had in common and how precious the ties of our faith are. May this be the beginning of a better understanding among us, and a more devoted brotherliness that will bring us into a unity that grows out of a faith in Christ our Lord!

The last days in Holland took me into several of the homes of our Dutch friends who received me so hospitably and treated me so kindly that it was difficult to feel like a stranger. Then one forenoon the international train took me across the border into Belgium and on to the Alsatian land where autumn was beginning to display its colors and decorate itself in preparation for the European winter.

X

WHERE THE GHOSTS WALK

There are very few people who have not had experiences during their lifetime that bring figures out of the "shadows" and set them to walking again. Some of these happenings may have been sorrowful and tragic, others perhaps were filled with joy and carry with them happy memories. One such incident is reflected in the following lines penned by Henry Wadsworth Longfellow, Harvard's great professor of English Literature, and one of America's foremost poets. One summer night his wife appeared on the platform of Mechanic's Hall in Boston to give a reading before a large assembly of people. A gust of wind from the backstage blew her dress into the flame of the footlights which resulted in burns from which she died. Years afterward when her bereaved companion sat by the fireside in the evening dusk, he saw her, in his reverie, coming out of the past and taking the chair beside him as she used to before this tragedy occurred. Then words began to flow and he gave to the world one of his most touching and tender poems:

FOOTSTEPS OF ANGELS

When the hours of day are numbered
    And the voices of the night
Wake the better soul that slumbered,
    To a holy, calm delight;

Ere the evening lamps are lighted,
    And, like phantoms grim and tall,
Shadows from the fitful firelight
    Dance upon the parlor wall;

Then the forms of the departed
Enter at the open door,
The beloved, the true-hearted,
Come to visit me once more.

* * *

And with them the being beauteous
Who unto my youth was given,
More than all things else to love me,
And is now a saint in heaven.

With a slow and noiseless footstep
Comes that messenger divine
Takes the vacant chair beside me,
Lays her gentle hand in mine.

And she sits and gazes at me
With those deep and tender eyes,
Like the stars, so still and saint-like
Looking downward from the skies.

Such an experience can never be forgotten even though it occurred within peaceful surroundings with no malicious forethought on the part of anyone. However sad the incident itself may have been there were factors connected with it that no doubt brought comfort and consolation to those who were left of the family and friends. But such is not always the case. The world today is filled with sorrows and suffering of proportions hitherto unmatched, tragedies that grew out of human terror and devastation, in which one can find nothing that time will heal nor the years can mollify. Feelings have been outraged and spirits wounded beyond repair, save by the grace and goodness of God.

People who saw all that they cherished—family, friends, homes, and possessions—disappear when armies swept over them like a flood or when bombers roared out of the sky and dropped missiles of death and destruction upon them, cannot banish from their minds the memories that rise out of such experiences. Often, too, they saw their wives and daughters raped and ravished and their children killed or wounded beyond any hope of healing. Such scenes will not soon be forgotten, and when the evening comes and the noises of the day die down then the "Ghosts begin to walk" and they see again the terrible things that happened to those whom they loved.

The people of a quaint old Wüttemberg city, rich in the lore of the past, will never forget the December night when fire fell upon them from beyond the clouds. It happened at the time of day when offices and shops were about to close. The streets were filled with people hurrying homeward from their work. The tensions, occasioned by the lurking dangers that are always present in wartime, were probably somewhat tempered by the spirit of the approaching Christmas season which means so much to the people of that romantic region. Suddenly the air was alive with planes swarming overhead and bombs, phosphorescent bombs, began to fall. Buildings were blown to pieces. Flames leaped skyward while the city burned. Whatever anticipations they may have had of a homey evening by their firesides, or of rest and quietness with their families, were gone. Throughout the night those who survived battled with the fires, cared for the wounded, and sought to rescue the crippled or dead from this burning cauldron. When their losses were counted some twenty to thirty thousand were found missing. Who can reckon or compute such a loss in which is included not only the property that was destroyed or the people who perished or those who were hopelessly maimed, but also the things that happened to the minds and souls of those who escaped physical injury? What a night to remember! What scenes, shrieks of terror, cries of helplessness, visions of dying children or fathers or mothers to haunt a person during the remainder of a lifetime!

Some five years later when I visited this place much of the rubble had been cleared away. Here and there buildings had been restored, and others were under construction or in the process of being repaired. The dead, except for such as had not been recovered from the wreckage, were laid away in long, large graves on the hillside outside of the city. People went to and fro from work from early morning until late in the evening trying to rebuild their homes and places of business and to lift again their city above its ruins and desolation.

Close by the place where I slept stood what was left of an old church. Sections of its walls and part of the belfry were still standing. During the night I was awake and sat for some time on the hard church bench which constituted my bed. The darkness was filled with a quiet peace. Moonlight fell through the broken windows and gave them the appearance of great, ghoulish eyes like those of some nocturnal wanderer who had returned from the "shades." The occasional rustling of leaves in the pitiful remnant of what was one time a tree near by, sounded like the sighing of imprisoned souls—maybe some were still embedded in the rubble! I lay back again to resume my rest but here so near to one of the great tragedies of warfare, sleep seemed forbidden. I fancied that I heard the roar of bombers and saw the flash of antiaircraft guns. In my thoughts I tried to visualize the night of the city's disaster, the wild panic, the fierce rage of strong men as they saw the work of generations disappear, and the helpless despair of those who were beyond the reach of human aid. At places like this it is easy to lose one's self in reverie and conjure up strange imaginations, here where the ghosts walk.

But it is not only the centers, where munitions or implements of war are produced or where military might resides or the strategy of war is being planned, that are laid low before the encroachment of armies or destruction administered from air or sea. Often peaceful villages, unarmed and harmless people, are made to suffer for reasons which make one wonder. One of the villages in Alsace where I visited was four times caught in the paths of contending armies. When peace finally came and the inhabitants, such as were left, returned to what was once their place of abode, they stared upon ravaged fields and desolate home sites. Perhaps during the rest of their days they will hear in their dreams the roar of the conflict and feel again the anguish they felt in those troubled days.

No story I heard was more touching than that of a village girl who lived in the beautiful vine-covered hills of the Palatinate, in the Rhineland. It happened on a Sunday when the Sabbath calm and peace brooded over the countryside. People had returned from church and wives were occupied with preparing the usual Sunday noon meal. This daughter of a widowed mother was sent to the village well for water and became engrossed with watching a plane that soared so gracefully and beautifully over them, high up in the sky. It looked like a great bird, she said, with wings of silver which glittered in the sun as it sailed back and forth over them. Hastening to the house she called her mother to come and see how prettily and leisurely it floated through the air. Then it disappeared in the distant cloud and was lost to view. Heeding her mother's counsel she closed the door and kept away from the windows. In a short time the incident was dismissed until suddenly the warning bomb fell outside the city. Then the air swarmed with planes and fire was literally rained from the sky. When the raid was over houses had been blown to bits or were aflame and the wreckage was strewn far and wide. The maimed, wounded, dead, and dying lay everywhere. The home of this mother and her children was left intact and the family unhurt. Even now I think of the words this young woman used in her effort to describe the wild fear that seized upon them when they stood in the shadow of death. When war comes everybody understands that it knows no mercy, that industrial centers must be wrecked, military stores destroyed, and armies blasted to pieces. But these folks, who fell into none of these categories, will always wonder what they had done that this had to happen to them. In daytime toil and care occupy their minds and tax their energy. They, like all the people of devastated lands are engaged in a struggle for food, for shelter and the other necessities of life. But in the stilly darkness when the winds sigh and the sounds of night rule the world then "the ghosts walk" again.

The greatest and most pathetic tragedies of war are not blasted buildings, demolished industries, or disorganized economic or political systems, serious and terrible as all of those are, but the human wreckage—the backwash of the war, some from the slime pits and gutters of sin. Here you will find men and women, crippled in body and soul, for whom life means only emptiness. There are widows who will have to travel life's way alone, some with children forced upon them by men wild with lust at a time when all moral restraints are gone. There are homeless, abandoned children, many of which were unwanted before they were born. Some of them will always be handicapped or suffer from designs upon their lives before they ever saw the light of day. Who is there that can reckon the spiritual loss, the mental anguish, and the physical suffering of those who fell into the clutches of, or are the offspring of, lust-hungry men.

I recall having heard a noted University President speak before a large convocation of students in 1922. Among the things he said was the striking statement that war is immoral. When the trumpets begin to blow, he said, all the normal restraints that ordinarily govern human conduct naturally disappear. At that time this seemed to me like a strong assertion. Some of us, even now, like to think that during such great upheavals as the world has passed through in the last thirty-five years there are those who want to think right. But when we study the history of events that followed we are forced to the conclusion that the least and the most one can say in behalf of the case is that principles of righteousness are forced to take a greatly subordinated place. In 1939 when Hitler's forces crashed across Europe and finally drew the whole world into the conflict, a noted journalist trying to stem the war hysteria that was again rising said among other things that "all war is atrocious," but added that not all the atrocity stories are true. He warned his readers that the first casualty is always truth. During this last struggle it was demonstrated again that nations engaged in a deadly combat, in which their very existence is at stake, will not go by the rules of a book, nor will they be guided by the decisions of a referee.

Does one wonder, then, why moral disorders such as would not be condoned in times of peace often prevail, and that men mad with illicit desires roam the streets and prey upon womanhood to find satisfaction for their carnality? Moral disorder is the greatest casualty of war! Buildings can be replaced, industries restored, and business resumed. Barren or shell pocked fields within a few years will again yield their harvests, the vineyards their wine, and the trees their fruit; but broken bodies, minds, and souls can not be so easily mended or restored.

The one shining spot in a world so torn by strife and filled with hate and bitterness is the work of those relief agencies that followed the armies and rendered such wide and impartial service to friend and foe. In this time of great and unparalleled need they gathered food for the hungry, clothes and shoes for the destitute, and made attempts to provide homes for the homeless. No one can ever know what these efforts, though often scanty and inadequate, must have meant to suffering people in the day of their sorrow and helplessness. But following the injunction of the Saviour and His apostles these ambassadors of good will mustered not only the things required for the physical bodies but tried also to mobilize all the resources of Christian love and kindness and sympathy and weave them into their work of charity as they bestowed their gifts upon people of all lands and nations. It will require volumes to tell the story of what these messengers of mercy did. Only the grateful hearts of those who benefited from it will know in its deepest sense the meaning of what the Master had in mind when He said, "it is more blessed to give than to receive." Those who left homes filled with comfort, stood in the chilling morning atmosphere of an alien, perhaps an enemy land, slept in unheated rooms, they understand. Over many of those who came for help hung the shadow of a lost husband or father who disappeared in the conflict or a mother who was lost in the shuffle, or little children—brothers and sisters maybe—who became separated when the warm little handclasp that had held them together let go at the time one or the other faltered and fell by the way.

During the war and afterward some of these drifting waifs were gathered into homes and cared for by those whose hands and hearts had been made warm and tender by divine grace. In southern France some of the little refugees from the Spanish Revolution together with orphans from France were gathered into one of these homes of refuge. Many will no doubt remember to the end of their days the love and help they received there. Among them were a little boy and girl, brother and sister, who became separated from the rest of their family but clung to each other in their wanderings until they found their way to a relief center from which they were sent to this home. Heerewegen, a beautiful country place in Holland, was requisitioned and turned over to the Mennonite Central Committee. Here children were cared for in the time of Holland's greatest need. In Belgium, just outside of Brussels, was another one of these homes operated by people who had no resources except their faith which God honored by moving their friends to provide the means whereby the work could be carried on. The Weiler Children's Home is located in a beautiful hill country near the German border on the French side of the Rhine. It has an established record for its noble service to the children of that area. For a number of years it was under the direction and control of the Mennonite Central Committee. Recently the buildings and grounds were purchased by the French Mennonites who will carry it on as a permanent project. A home for the larger children was earlier maintained at Nancy. This good work was recently closed and was moved to Belfort where other aspects of the needs of the people are emphasized.

At the Babies' Home near Brussels there were at the time of my visit some twenty to thirty homeless ones whose mothers were unable to provide for them or did not want them. Many had fathers who did not know of their existence. As the matron related briefly the case history of each one, we were made to wonder how children coming from lives so corrupt as some of them did, could be so sweet and lovable and pleasant. In one of the cribs lay a helpless one, without a mind, old enough to romp and play, but who will never walk because of what happened to it before it was born. They say there are many such. Another little girl almost smiled herself out of her little chair as she seemingly tried to make herself acceptable to her caretaker and to the visitors. Perhaps she was trying to find a father and mother who would give her a place in their hearts and bestow upon her their love and affections. Unwanted little waifs of the world's upheaval they are! But "of such," said the Saviour, "is the kingdom of heaven." How beautiful they are in their innocency; but all too soon they will grow into the years where they must travel the long road alone and face a world that is harsh and often unkind. May God show them the way and keep them as they go!

Those who were sheltered in these homes are the fortunate ones. But on the outside there is a great host of them. Some are cared for in their homes as little ones normally are. Many were unwanted—children of unleashed passion—but when they came their mothers opened their hearts and gave them their love. Others are dependent upon charitable organizations who put them into such hands as are willing to provide for them as they can. One hears of other mothers who hate the child that was imposed upon her by its father who was from an enemy country, and who at a time of mad revelry was told the "day is yours— and the night." What else can we expect? And yet the situation of these helpless little ones haunted me. I wished that their fathers could be found and some court would impose upon them the penalty of searching out the little ones for whose existence they are responsible and then force them to witness the plight into which they have placed them. Maybe they too would see "ghosts walk" the rest of their days. I had just come to Genoa, Italy, from one of these homes where I had listened to some of these sad stories. Somehow the voice of a crying infant, across the street from the hotel where I stayed that night, kept me from sleeping. I wondered whether it was one of those unloved little ones who was even from its cradle making its way alone without the affection of parents or friends!

"V" days came, when they said, "the war is over." Then with colors flying and drums beating, long lines of victorious men marched in victory parades along streets lined with applauding multitudes. But the war was not over, nor is it yet, nor will it be when fighting ceases or when buildings are reconstructed, industries rehabilitated and cities rebuilt. Not until the human wreckage has been salvaged and redeemed and has found a constructive place in society, will the war be over.

Of course this is Germany, and people will say, "She had it coming." When one looks over the acres of ruins in London, in Belgium, in Holland, and in France or Germany, he cannot by any stretch of the imagination be impressed with any evidence of generosity or goodness on the part of any of the military powers that wrought such destruction of life and property. The only conclusion that one can arrive at is that war can never be endued with Christian acts or graces or with what one considers humanitarian deeds or motives. It is now what it always was and always will be—a relapse to acts of savagery in order to attain one's ends—and any nation or people that resorts to such measures to adjust its grievances or satisfy its ambitions will have to be ready to take what goes with it.

In the two global conflicts in which our country participated it was spared the devastation and destruction of life and property that fell to the lot of people over whose territory contending armies swept. This will not happen again. If and when such an holocaust should take place it will come to our doors and we will be called upon to share all the harrowing experiences that other nations did in the past. During my travels in the stricken countries I took but few pictures of the wreckage. The piles of rubble, the miles of demolished buildings may be photographed, but the mass of it looks so immeasurably insignificant when reduced to a 35 mm. slide. Even if it were possible to adequately reproduce it on paper, the most important element, the human, would still be missing. No camera, no painter's brush, no words in any language can reproduce or describe that which takes place inside of a person when flames begin to fall or when buildings are blown to atoms or when people die as they do on fields of battle or in bomb-blasted cities.

When I left home it was summertime. The fields were whitening to harvest. Corn leaves were rustling, the trees were green and the pastures were filled with herds that grazed leisurely the lush grasses or lay by the streams at noontide like harvesters taking their rest. I thought I had never seen the country more beautiful nor did our homes ever look more peaceful. I felt it a privilege and a joy to be alive. Cities along the way were clean and bustling with life and energy. New York, great monster by the sea, raised high its massive head, beset with its jagged crown. It almost seemed that one could feel the throb of its roar and its power even before it came into sight. Cargo ships destined for other lands lined the water front. A thrill rose in my soul as we sailed past the Statue of Liberty with torch held aloft—a symbol of the freedom of which our nation is supposed to be the champion. As the skyline dropped out of sight I stood by the rail watching it go down and was deeply thankful for such a homeland.

It was not until I reached Le Havre on the coast of France that I saw the first evidences of war. It is when one follows the road of destruction through London and other places in Britain or halts where the Battle for France raged, and goes on through Luxembourg or stops at Rotterdam, Cologne, Hamburg, and all the other centers where military might and power was concentrated, that he realizes how devastatingly destructive modern warfare really is. The ugly trail of what happens at times when people do their worst to each other reached all the way across Europe down to Italy's toe. At the time of my visit most of the disabled tanks, the wrecked trucks, jeeps and other vehicles and implements of war that had been strewn along the road or that littered the countryside had been removed. But acres covered with this battered equipment and junk appeared here and there. When I saw day by day the devastation that marked the path of Patton's army across Luxembourg and Germany and that of the Allies on every front, I was profoundly thankful that it had not happened to us but I could not help wondering whether we were worthy of being spared the hardships and losses that had been imposed upon others.

Is "peace, and good neighborliness among men" too much to hope for in our day of enlightenment, scientific achievement, schools, churches and all the organizations and machinery of various kinds that have been designed to alleviate human suffering and build up good will among men? Somehow the resources that looked so hopeful to us a half century ago have failed, and instead of the fruits we had anticipated—peace, equality, justice, and love among men—we live in a world with insatiable desires, rivalry, jealousy, greed, and inequality that has poisoned the very atmosphere we breathe and built up walls of hatred and ill will instead.

As we keep on admiring our advancements in knowledge and our accomplishments along industrial lines we all at once become aware of their inadequacy as long as human nature remains what it is—unregenerate and unsanctified. So long as the statesmanship of our day is narrowed by prejudice and lack of justice, and diplomacy is seasoned with intrigue and the spirit of nations is rooted in selfishness, we need little wonder that the world has gone awry.

May we then pray that our civilization, which seems to be at the point of sinking under the weight of its mistakes, of its good intentions wrongly based, and its fallacious concepts of what it needs, may we pause and humbly confess its vanity and its sins. And above all may the saints of God arise, clothed in the armor of their might, and show to all men by their faith and their way of life, the great resources of power that reside in the Unseen with whom we all have to do. Some of us are simple enough of mind to believe that is where the answer is to be found. This task will not be easy. It will be filled with hardship and discouragements and frequently with seeming defeat. But often before our time the destiny of a people and a cause was hinged on the faith of the few. It may be again. The forces of righteousness have ever been in the minority. They are now. Let us then be true to what we believe, and faithful in the things committed unto us until the day of the Great Illumination when at His coming time will be brought to an end and out of the smoke of a dissolving universe will come a new heaven and a new earth in which righteousness will dwell. Then we shall see all things in their proper perspective and "we shall know as we are known" and then—the ghosts will walk no more!

XI

FROM VENICE TO BOMBAY

One afternoon in late September a gondola drew up in front of the Continental Hotel in the city of Venice to take passengers to the dock where they were to embark for Bombay, India, or points en route. Our pilot propelled his little craft with a skill that only Venetians know. The days of waiting under dripping skies did not inspire too many regrets when the time of departure came. The ship was scheduled to sail at 3:00 P.M. but for some reason it did not appear in port until six. Consequently we enjoyed the bliss of sitting on the hard benches of the customs house until its arrival. In London where the reservations were made we were informed that the vessel on which we were to sail was new. When we saw it, it had all the appearance of newness. Later information, gleaned en route, revealed the fact that it was in reality an old one which had sailed between Italy and Alexandria for more than a quarter of a century. During the war it had come in line with a submarine missile and went to the bottom of the sea. Since then it was raised from its grave and rebuilt entirely. Its cabins, dining room, and lounge were beautifully finished and except for being loaded to the limit of its capacity it offered us the prospect of a pleasant voyage.

An obliging porter took me to my cabin. I was pleased with the location. It was on the deck near the center. Two small windows instead of portholes, assured us of good ventilation and fresh air. All seemed well except that I wondered how three persons could comfortably occupy a "cubbyhole" so small. As I sat pondering the prospect an English-speaking official of the company entered, closed the door behind him and in utmost secrecy informed me that a serious mistake had been made. I wondered what I had done. Visions of being stranded in Italy with no prospect of getting reservations for months or perhaps languishing in one of Mussolini's prisons for having innocently violated some law began to loom up before me. I immediately recalled stories of atrocities in Nazi, Fascist, and Soviet jails and of difficulties in getting released. Judging by my name (which I thought was unmistakably Pennsylvania Dutch), he said they had concluded that I was an Indian. Therefore they had assigned two persons who they thought were my countrymen to share the remaining space with me. His apologies were profuse as Latin apologies always are. At once my anxieties subsided and my breathing again became normal. I was given the choice of rooming with them for the twenty-five-day duration of the voyage or accepting a berth in a cabin below the deck which was to be occupied by a retired British engineer, and a Franciscan friar from Pittsburgh, Pennsylvania, en route to India as a missionary. Acting on the advice of the officer I chose the latter alternative which I soon regretted. This room was smaller, closer to the water line and had only one porthole for ventilation. But the decision was made and I determined to make the best of it. The gong brought all the first-class passengers—forty-six in number, together for our table assignment and the first meal. As the ship sailed out of the harbor into the sea we had the pleasure of meeting for the first time those who were to be our neighbors during the trip.

A summary inventory of the passengers who assembled in the dining room indicated a mixed crowd. There was a young Indian businessman and his bride, both Christians, who had been married in the U.S.A. where she was attending State College at Lansing, Michigan. He had been sent to America on a purchasing trip for a large firm in Bombay. There was a Danish nurse on the way to South India to take charge of a Lutheran hospital. An Austrian lady with two children was en route to join her husband. Beside the Franciscan friar from Pittsburgh there were four Italians who belonged to the same Brotherhood, also on the way to their mission field north of Calcutta. The rest of our group consisted mostly of Anglo-Indians who had gone to England hoping to live on their pensions but were now returning to their native land, disillusioned and unhappy—some of them—over their future which seemed none too bright. Then there was a group of Indian students who had been in attendance at universities and colleges on the continent, in England, or the United States, who were also on the way home, not too sure of their future because of the radical changes that had taken place during their sojourn abroad. Beside the friars there was a bevy of six nuns who belonged to a teaching order of the church. They were going to South India to teach in the mission schools.

Passengers on shipboard are always interesting though not all of them are inspiring. However, one was deeply impressed with the quiet decorum, orderliness, devotion and friendliness of the sisters. I much desired to secure a picture of this somberly clad, well-behaved group. One of the Fathers informed me that it would be allowable. Upon my insistence he made inquiry only to be informed that their vows forbade all forms of vanity including that of posing for photos. He suggested taking it on the sly. I could well visualize the scowl of disapproval upon the benign face of the "Mother" in charge and the expression of horror on the countenances of all of them should I be caught in such an attempt. I felt that if there was anyone left whose convictions led them to honor a religious vow that their sincerity should be respected. Hence they are not included in my collection of Kodachromes. The Brothers, however, were less conscientious. They had no scruples about having their pictures taken. They—all except the one from Pittsburgh—indulged freely in the current pastimes with which the passengers occupy themselves. At least one of them was on speaking terms with the Pope. From him, during one of our conversations, I acquired

106

advance information of the "Holy Father's" intention of calling a convocation of the Bishops of the church in 1950 for the purpose of confirming the Dogma of the Assumption of the Virgin Mary. This being "Holy Year" it was thought an appropriate time.

Beside those described there was the "mine-run" of passengers from all walks of life. Some were Hindus, others Mohammedans, a few were Christians. The hold was filled with boy scouts and their masters from Pakistan who were returning from a summer trip to the Scandinavian countries. They were steerage passengers but they overran the entire ship and occupied the best places everywhere except at the table. They complained of poor food and insufficient quantities. This precipitated a strike one day and for a time it looked as though it might become serious. There was talk among the passengers that some of the leaders might be put in chains and locked up for the duration of the voyage. During their travels all summer long they were treated with consideration. Now they occupied the lowest place. This was too much for those who had just come into possession of a country of their own after having been a people among people for centuries. But when they clashed with the officers of the ship they met in the person of the Captain a man, who not only looked like Mussolini but who had the iron will of the dictator when he was at his height. After several meetings with the scoutmasters and their leaders the storm subsided. They learned at least one lesson that led them to realize that freedom does not mean that everyone can do as he wishes regardless of how it affects others.

Owing to the limited deck space there was no swimming pool. Deck games such as shuffleboard, table tennis, and kindred sports that usually occupy such a large place on most ships were wanting on this one. Hence the bar and card tables were filled from morning until evening. For the most part the voyage was uneventful except for the excitement two little five-year-olds—

one an Austrian, the other the child of an English lady—furnished by hanging precariously over the railing of the ship until our good Danish nurse took matters in hand. Then they hibernated in one or the other's cabins and passed their waking hours playing with their mothers' matches and cigarettes while the latter spent their time at the bar with their "gentlemen" friends. One day while these little girls were occupied with their routine entertainment the curtains at the cabin window were set aflame and nearly caused a fire at sea. The reprimand which the Captain gave these two ladies in public was a classic and worth the discomfort of an ocean voyage on a two-thousand-ton liner to listen to. I never knew that an officer whose language, however noble the theme, was usually seasoned with expletives, superfluous adjectives, adverbs, modifying phrases and clauses, could so completely eliminate all the unnecessary terms and constructions and deliver such a worthy piece of hortatory art. For several days the mothers smarted, I presume, from the stinging rebuke, then they again appeared at the bar as usual, clad in their hot weather regalia to assume their former associations and occupations.

Coming down the Adriatic Sea the ship sailed along the coast. The cooling breezes of the Mediterranean offered us much comfort after the heat on the mainland. The little library freshly stocked with new books provided good reading material and afforded some of us many pleasant hours. The first stop was at Brindisi, an important seaport of the Ancient Roman Empire. Here Paul would likely have landed had their captain heeded the apostle's advice. But when the storm had carried them far out of their course and tossed them hither and yon until their vessel went to pieces, they found one from Alexandria that took them to Puteoli on the opposite side of Italy. A few blocks from the docks stood an old marble shaft which marked the eastern terminus of the Appian Way. The inscription in Latin informed us that this great military highway was completed in 312 B.C.

Today, after millenniums have passed, it still stands though its base is now held secure with iron bands.

Here, too, I saw women, treading in Biblical fashion with bare feet, the grapes in the wine vats—good wine they said, which passengers on board ship drank by the jugful. Evidently this grape treading is a feminine occupation in Brindisi. The loaded clusters bursting beneath their feet stained their limbs and saturated their clothing until they looked like the blood-soaked garments of which Isaiah speaks when in visions he saw the man coming up from Edom striding along with his cloak clinging to his legs as he walked.

Who is this that cometh from Edom, with dyed garments from Bozrah? This that is glorious in his apparel, travelling in the greatness of his strength?

I that speak in righteousness, mighty to save.

Wherefore art thou red in thine apparel, and thy garments like him that treadeth in the winefat?

I have trodden the winepress alone . . . and their blood shall be sprinkled upon my garments.

Isaiah 63:1-3

Here in this old, old city we spent an entire day walking its streets, sitting at its sidewalk tables in front of cafes, while the Brindisian world went by.

This was to be our last stopping place at an occidental port. Sometime during the night the ship was loosed from its moorings and when morning came no land was to be seen. We were floating on the bosom of the great waterway of the ancients. Vessels from Solomon's navy and from the merchant fleets of the Phoenicians coursed across this vast sea long before people knew of the lands where you and I were born. When the merchant-men of the Royal Navy returned from their three-year cruise to Tarshish they were loaded with gold and silver, ivory, apes, and peacocks. One day the sailors pointed out to us the isle of Crete where Paul on his journey to Rome urged the master of his ship to stop for the winter. Then all traces of land were lost again until one day the shoreline of Egypt appeared along the horizon and sometime later we drew up to the docks at Port Said.

When a foreign steamer enters an Egyptian port, policemen, properly and impressively armed, come on board and take command of affairs. After the elaborate routine of formal bowing and salutations was over, and the customs officials and officers of the ship had leisurely and amply satiated their thirst with Italian wine and eaten their lunch together, they betook themselves to their duties. Cameras were forbidden. Passengers were warned beforehand that all mail received or posted here would be opened. Those who wanted to go ashore were granted permits provided they were willing to deposit their passports with the immigration officers until their return from the trip through the city. Here we found some beautiful shops and lovely streets, a host of unprincipled vendors and the most disgusting beggars I have ever seen. It is, however, not at all necessary to leave the ship in order to do shopping. No sooner had it cast its anchor than boatloads of merchandise in charge of skilled salesmen drew up alongside and a bedlam of bargaining ensued. This is the beginning of the Orient as far as business tactics and practices of salesmanship go.

From Port Said to Suez, a city at the lower terminus of the Suez Canal, vessels are always in charge of government pilots who know the way. Somewhere to the west from where we were the Israelites spent some four hundred years of their existence on the Delta of the Nile where they had settled at Joseph's behest. Here they became farmers instead of herdsmen. In this environment their entire way of life was changed. Somewhere along our route is where they crossed the "Sea of Reeds"—the Red Sea—on the night when a strong east wind parted the waters and they passed over into the desert. From that place they saw the Egyptians flounder and drown in the returning flood while the wide spaces rang with the shouts of the men and the songs of the women led by Miriam. Day after day as we sailed onward, the eastern shore was visible in the murky atmosphere. Spots of interest were pointed out by the friars who had gone up and down this route many times. At Jeddah the Pakistanis swarmed along the rail. Back from here lies Mecca, the shrine of the Mohammedans. They told us this is where Eve found her last resting place. If this is correct then she had wandered far from her original habitat—there is no evidence of anything like a paradise within miles from here.

This is the shore along which the Israelites marched on their way to Sinai. As one travels in the heat of the Red Sea, he can well understand why they should have despaired. A person can imagine the emotions of these people who came from the low, flat Delta lands when the lofty mountains in the distance first came into view. What awe they felt then must have melted into fear on the morning when Sinai "burned like a furnace" and God spoke to them out of the clouds. This whole area is historic ground, held almost sacred by the followers of the three great monotheistic religious of our time. All three received their codes of law and rules of conduct from this section of the world. The Ten Commandments came to Israel at Sinai, the Sermon on the Mount was given to the Christians somewhere in Palestine and the Koran of the Mohammedans came from their founder in Mecca of Arabia.

One hot, sultry morning the sailors informed us that sometime the following night or the next day we would arrive at Aden, the hottest place on earth. With many misgivings everyone awaited the time of arrival only to find much to their satisfaction that the friendly breeze which sprang up the previous afternoon continued throughout our stop in this port, and provided for us a pleasant stay at this otherwise barren and desolate place. This area is under British control. Here one sees order, discipline, and cleanliness as it is administered by expert colonial masters. Even beggars and overly solicitous taxi drivers move

111

when told to do so by officers, English or native, who stand loyally "For the Queen and for the Country."

This is where the old and the new, the Orient and the Occident, come together. Women with veiled faces, dressed in long, somber, flowing garments walk side by side with those clad in modern array—including women in shorts! The streets are filled with every known kind of vehicle or mode of transportation—taxis, busses, automobiles, camel carts, camel trains, bicycles, carts, coaches, and donkeys. The show room of the Ford Agency was filled with shiny cars of the latest models, including Mercurys, and perhaps one or so Lincolns. In front of this display was parked a camel hitched to a cart such as probably brought Abraham to Haran and Palestine. In the shops along the street there were on sale all the cosmetics, curios, Swiss watches, novelties, etc., that are to be found in the places where tourists, travelers, and sailors stop. The first contingent of women who went ashore incidentally came across a good supply of hosiery of a kind difficult to secure in England and not available in India. This was their last opportunity to replenish this section of their wardrobe. Like the two spies of Joshua's day, they returned with a good report. This touched off a shopping "spree." As soon as the places of business opened for the afternoon trade the ladies, some anxious and excited swarmed over the side of the ship, clambered into the motor boats and made for the shore. When they came back that evening they had the nylons and the merchants had the money. Judging from the remarks one heard during the evening and the next few days, these itinerant shoppers had fared very well.

A trip across the mountain took us to Crater, a city at the foot of the mountain with a wide, dreary desert expanse stretching eastward. We came here late in the afternoon and found the streets filled with people, goats, donkeys, dogs, and now and then a cow. En route the guide pointed out to us the traditional site of the grave where Cain is said to be buried. Coming back from

Crater to Aden we followed a road that led us through a tunnel which at the time was choked with a train of mule camels that evidently enjoyed the coolness of this retreat and decided to stay. Such noises as the agitated drivers made should have set the whole outfit in motion but for a time all effort seemed unavailing. After the passageway was finally cleared we proceeded to the Queen of Sheba's Garden and "Wells" which consisted of a series of large reservoirs on which the good queen depended for the water supply for her household, her gardens and her grounds.

But one wonders when it ever rained sufficiently to fill these tanks. At the present rate of precipitation it would take more than two hundred years the weathermen say. These wells as they are called are marvels of engineering skill. A whole series of them lie between the mountains surrounding the city. No one knows when they were built. If the traditions regarding them are true, then they are as old, or older, than Solomon's day. For centuries dust blown from the desert accumulated until they were entirely filled and their presence forgotten. Some years ago one of the British officials found some traces of masonry protruding above the soil. His investigations led to the discovery of these unusual remnants of an earlier culture which after much effort were finally completely excavated and restored. The Mohammedan tradition regarding the Queen of Sheba's residence at this place is questionable although the reservoirs indicate that at some time there must have been extensive cultural developments here. Neither does the tradition of Cain's grave high up in the mountains at Steamer Point or Eve's burial at Jeddah have any foundation in fact, however stoutly the guides who show tourists around defend the truthfulness of their statements.

One wonders where people in desolate places like this get their food. The shops seemed to be well stocked—even fresh fruit and some vegetables were on display. The goats, pigs, donkeys, chickens, children, and grownups looked fairly well fed.

While we were pondering the problem a camel train loaded with hay, melons, onions, oranges, grapes, and such things as fill the shelves of the store and the larders of the kitchen came from somewhere on the back side of the desert where these things grow. Little oases watered by springs fed by the melting snows on far distant mountains give life to these barren places where people's wants are few and having food and raiment they are therewith content. Beautiful homes dot the hillsides where the British colonial officers and alien businessmen live. At Crater there is a Danish Lutheran Mission. A clergyman who has charge of the Anglican Church at Aden came on board to "catch a breath of Europe," he said. I do not know whether he was satisfied with what he got. Mission work among these Arabians, he assured us, is very difficult.

Here at Aden is located the terminus of the pipe lines that reach to the oil fields far back in the desert. The Red Sea is full of tankers that carry this "black gold" to distant ports to supply the gas hunger of many countries. When the sun was going down I got into a motorboat filled with guards that patrol the lines and stand by the huge tanks spread along the shores and causeways in the harbor. They were a jolly, rollicking set, armed with dangerous weapons ready for any emergency their duty might thrust upon them during the lonely hours of the night. A few of them understood or spoke English. Most of the time they jabbered in their own tongue and seemed pleased to have an American civilian on board their little craft. This small corner was apparently one of the spots where people did not suffer from the effects of American charity, politically dispensed. They have oil to sell and they still like us. In our company, too, was an irate Arab who on orders from his spouse was trying to deliver a bundle of bedding she had prepared for a son who was on board a ship sailing out of the harbor. With shouts and gesticulations that would have impressed anyone but a sea captain, he made his requests known and finally when the vessel

114

was brought to a stop at a fueling station he relieved himself of his burden. This short cruise in the harbor of Aden enabled me to secure some comprehension of the enormous place that oil holds in the affairs of nations. Across the mouth of the Suez Canal, on the Egyptian side, is another storage and shipping center covering acres and acres of ground. The great tanks look impressive, almost attractive, against the background of bleak, low mountains. A few trees in the foreground give evidence of an attempt to add some little touches of hominess to these otherwise barren places.

After dark we left Aden for Karachi, a seaport of Pakistan where a few of the former British colonial officers remained as straggling remnants of a vanishing order of things. Here we felt for the first time the bitterness that exists between the Mohammedans and the Hindus. The non-Moslem Indians that sailed with us were extremely reluctant to venture beyond the limits of the port except in the company of Europeans or Americans. Sprawling along the shore was a large group of buildings once occupied by American soldiers who were brought here to become seasoned and conditioned for service in India. These buildings, we were told, are now used to house refugees that have come out of the Mohammedan-Hindu debacle. Another five days of sailing brought us to Bombay, the end of our voyage, the gateway to India, the land and people of hope and dreams, many of which have yet to be realized.

XII

HAIL, INDIA

It was near sundown on October 25, 1949, when our ship sailed into the harbor of Bombay. Before us stood one of the large cities of the world. Malabar Hill to our left raised its lovely, tree-crowned head high above its surroundings. Modern apartment houses lined the drive along the shore and the large commercial buildings to our right cast their evening shadows into the sea. The docks were crowded, they said, which meant that we were destined to swelter another night in our little cabin on shipboard. The cooks seem to have been in a good mood. They outdid themselves to give us a good last dinner. Everything was tasty and well prepared. Their supply of olive oil must have been low for the food came untainted with the taste or smell of it. By noon the next day the ship was maneuvered safely through the network of canals and the labyrinth of docks to the proper pier. From my position along the rail I recognized the welcome form of George Beare, one of the missionaries, who had come to meet me.

At last I stood on India's soil!—the land I had been in touch with for years through my connection with missions and missionaries. In fancy all kinds of imagery had been built up regarding the country, its people, its wealth, its poverty, and its life. Now I was to realize my dreams for the first time and actually see for myself what it was like. First in order was the ordeal of going through customs. My own belongings which were few passed without difficulty. But I had brought with me several rolls of Kodachrome film for a friend and a pair of glasses for another, and that's where our trouble started. On board ship I was advised to declare each article. This, as a matter of course, was the ethical thing to do. I was assured—almost—that the custom's officials would admit these little parcels without duty. India, however, needs money and here was an opportunity to acquire a few extra coins to replenish its waning stockpile of cash. We devoted the greater part of two and a half days going from office to office, waiting in lobbies, talking to officials and signing documents in order to secure the permits to enter these few small items which a person could have carried in his pocket without them being noticed. When we at last emerged from the customs house we had not only our diminutive parcels, but also a sheaf of papers including an importer's permit, and beside we had had conferences with important men before whom we tried to appear with proper decorum—humble and grateful for every favor. The government had some fifty additional rupees to put into its vaults.

Then began our trip around the city. We had rooms at Raj Mahal where the Brethren church maintains a Pension. Here travelers, especially missionaries, can find comfortable and pleasant sleeping quarters and get wholesome, well-prepared food served in family style. At the time of our stay in the city this place was in charge of Mr. and Mrs. Minnich, from the state of Indiana and from Tuscarawas County, Ohio, respectively. Not only were they good hosts but they were lovely people who at once made us feel that we had a home to come to.

This establishment stands as a witness of what the wise man had in mind when he said that bread cast upon the waters will return "after many days." Years ago when the Church of the Brethren established its work in India—so the story goes—a poor Mohammedan approached the mission for a loan to set up a small business for himself. With no security except this stranger's word, the transaction was made. Time passed by and this little affair became dim in the lender's mind or perhaps was forgotten. Years afterward a line of fine, new modern apartments arose along one of the best streets of Bombay and stretched out to the shoreline of the harbor. By this time the mission was contemplating the opening of a rooming house where incoming and outgoing workers of all denominations could find comfortable quarters and good board during their stay in the city and where others who come and go could find a congenial home during their sojourn. The owner of the "Raj Mahal" apartments was approached with the possibility of renting one floor of the building for such a purpose. Then he recalled the kindness and confidence of the mission folks in the days of his need and informed them that he had long hoped to be able to do something for the people who befriended him and started him on his road to wealth and success. The entire third floor was leased for a sum so small that it amounts to a fraction only of what he might realize from it. Missionaries, travelers, and all others who have enjoyed this little haven of rest and comfort in the great city of Bombay will always be grateful to this Mohammedan and also to those who touched his heart by their kindness and help in the day when he was in need.

I was now in India. The ordeal of customs house problems was over and we were established in comfortable quarters for the duration of our stay in the city. With these matters settled, one's mind was free to take stock of his surroundings. During my twenty-seven years in the office of secretary and president of the Mission Board I had been in close touch with India and its problems as they affected the missionaries, consequently I felt somewhat informed on its conditions and the ways of life of its people. When, however, I saw its cities and countryside, its jungles and villages, and its colorful throngs on the streets and highways and in the bazaars, I realized how little I really had grasped of what the country and its masses of humanity were like. On every side I saw new and interesting things and could not say that "everything looked like I thought it would."

Beare was a good guide. He knew the ways of the city, country, and jungle. Our first tour of observation was planned to take us several hundred miles up the coast to Ankleswar, where the Brethren Church has its mission headquarters. While waiting for transportation we spent the time going from place to place in the city. Our first trip took us to Malabar Hill, a beautiful residential district where the British officials lived when India was theirs, and where alien businessmen resided when they were the masters of its trade and commerce. Here in this land that knows no winter except in the highlands of the north, one sees what can be done in the way of landscaping. Shrubbery and flowers laid out in beautiful patterns cover the parks and lawns and line the sidewalks and streets.

Here a person needs to be prepared for new and strange things for this is the Orient with a culture that was hoary with age before ours began. Among the things that are unusual to us is the way in which the dead are disposed of. Christians bury underground as they do in the western lands, but in the Orient proper burial does not necessarily mean a lot in the cemetery and an appropriate service in the church and at the graveside. The Parsis leave the bodies to be consumed by the birds of the air. While coming up to Malabar Hill on a loaded bus we noticed a swarm of vultures gliding high above the trees and buildings. I was informed that over in their direction is "The Tower of Silence" where the dead are laid away. No sooner is a body placed on the elevated platform than these carrion eaters are on hand and within some fifteen to twenty minutes there is nothing left of the remains but the bare bones. At Calcutta we saw Hindus bring body after body into the crematory along the street where they were placed on piles of wood and burned. Sometimes one sees a few lonely, mournful people sitting by a burning pyre along some stream while the smoke of their departed ascends skyward. Strange customs, we think!

I have always heard of the beggars of India. I was prepared to see all kinds of demonstrations but I found them much the same as those of other lands. Some of them beg because it is the only way by which they can get food to eat. Others do it because they would rather do what a beggar has to do, and be what a beggar has to be, and get what a beggar gets, than to be what he has to be in order to hold a respectable job. Many of them, people say, have acquired wealth by means of their profession and have sizable bank accounts and real estate holdings. No doubt most of them have not fared so well and probably find it difficult to live on what they receive. There are all kinds of hopeless, helpless, pitiful creatures; impoverished, deformed, crippled, blind, and diseased that look to charitable hands for the things to live by and find their means meager enough.

The Indian people are deeply religious and have profound respect for things that are considered holy. In this category are cows and monkeys, neither of which gives evidence of innate moral sense in their conduct or attitude but become a tremendous burden upon the land that is always short of food. The sacred cows are worthless as far as marketable values go. They dare not be slaughtered and used for food hence they roam over the land and consume the grass on the wide open spaces or wander through the streets of the cities often interfering with traffic, poking their noses into shops and making off with such food as they can secure. These, together with other animals and pests which are tolerated for religious reasons, consume millions of tons of food that might otherwise be available for human consumption. The monkeys, of whom it is estimated there are not less than twenty-five million in the cultivated areas, consume one million tons of grain and destroy more than two million tons of foodstuff annually. To see these long-tailed fellows perform in the treetops or go scampering across the housetops and play almost humanlike may be amusing but when a person sees them hopping across the rice fields in droves or pulling down the fruit off the trees the humor of the situation changes, especially when hungry women and children have too little or nothing to eat.

However, the Indian people have reasons for dealing kindly with the monkey tribe. It figures largely in the story of their past. It reaches far back to where history is dim and perhaps more fanciful than real, more traditional than factual. Long ago, so the story goes, when men by mystical manipulations traveled through the air in chariots propelled by the paws and claws of animals (the forerunner of the airplane, perhaps!), the beautiful Sita, Queen wife of Ram, King of Ayodhya, was kidnaped from their forest retreat by the cruel ruler of the Island Kingdom of Ravanna. The narrator says that en route she dropped pearls along the way and threw her choicest strand into a cluster of monkeys sitting on a hilltop. By these means she was traced to the stronghold of her captor and rescued by an army of their tribe. No wonder they are granted all kinds of privileges! In the light of their valorous deeds of the past it may be well that their numbers should increase. India's future is ominous and foreboding enough to justify the mustering of all its resources of defense. It may need the services of these anthropoids again and their performance and behavior is in many ways as practical and helpful as the present-day "monkey shines" that pass for statescraft and statesmanship in circles you and I know.

India is a land of old tradition and practices that are deeply rooted in the past. To a person from the Western lands many of these are new but they carry with them something that is charming. I have never been enthusiastic about snake charmers and other magicians and voodoo people but they add something to the color of the country.

Somehow there is something beautiful about the way the people of India do their shopping. I do not have reference now to the haggling over prices that usually takes place when a North American tries to make purchases, but to the leisurely manner in which it is done. In the large markets the merchant and customer will likely sit down together. They may even serve refreshments while the bargaining is in progress. Porters, waiters, clerks, servants, or whatever they are called bring the articles for inspection and examination. When the purchase is made, the goods are deposited at a convenient place where porters pick them up and deliver them according to orders of the purchaser. If they are to go by train, they will be taken to the waiting room of the station where the buyer will hire a coolie to guard them until train time when porters pick them up and place them in the proper compartment. It is amazing what loads these people carry on their heads and for what a pittance they perform their tasks.

When North Americans speak about sleeping cars the well-appointed Pullman with carpeted floors, inner-spring mattresses, immaculate sheets, and neatly uniformed porters who come at the beck and call of the passengers, naturally come to mind. When my traveling companion spoke about "taking a sleeper" from Bombay to Raipur this is what I thought of, or rather I thought of nothing else. My surprise was complete when we entered our special compartment to find nothing but a board covered with leather which served the purpose of a seat for two in daytime and a bed at night. What padding or cushioning there was—if any—was so meager that it was not noticeable. Above was a similar board fixed on hinges to fold up against the wall in daytime if not needed for baggage and utilized at night for the upper berth. Here, too, the passengers furnish the bedding.

After having traveled twelve to fourteen hours without anything to eat one naturally wonders what to expect. George Beare had thoughtfully purchased a basket of oranges, tangerines, and bananas which served to satisfy our hunger, quench our thirst, and pass the time while en route. But still the wonder grew as to where coffee, eggs and toast which my stomach craved, might come from. There was no sign of a diner or newsboys that sold sandwiches en route. When the train came to a stop in front of the station a porter arrayed in dining room linen came along and took our order—just what was wanted—coffee, toast and eggs. Then the gong sounded, the conductor's whistle blew and the train was off on its journey. After a half hour or more—perhaps an hour—it came to a stop at another station and an exact replica of the porter who had taken our order appeared with the food which was most graciously served in our compartment. But long before we had finished the train moved on again leaving us with our half-eaten meal and trays in our laps. At the next stop a porter similarly arrayed relieved us of what was left —the trays, cups, and dishes. How different this is from our elaborate dining car service and yet what could be more acceptable than to have one's food served in the privacy of his own compartment even though it isn't lined with carpet or drapings or decorated with paintings.

What a surprise I had when I awoke the first morning and saw India as it was away from the large cities! I had heard and read about its jungles and always interpreted the word in accordance with impressions I received from my study of geography in my early grade school days. I thought of them as places where the trees dripped with moisture, of alligators and crocodiles wallowing in the dark, marshy swamps; of monkeys chattering in the treetops or swinging from the branches by their long tails and of huge snakes hanging down from the limbs above. Here in India the jungles are beautiful forests, rich with the color of flowering trees—often fragrant—and filled with birds of highly colored plumage among which is the peacock. Ever since the days of Solomon they have strutted through these lovely wilds displaying proudly their highly colored tail feathers just as they do now. Then there are winding roads with here and there a Hindu shrine, and crooked paths that lead to villages hidden deep within the shadows. I still wonder why it is or how it happened that these woods, so lovely, should be called by a name with such ugly connotations.

India, a land one third the size of the United States, has

more than two times its population, including that of its island possessions. In other words, if all the people of continental United States plus all those of its island possessions plus all the inhabitants of Canada would be moved into the U.S. territory east of the Mississippi River and then multiplied by two the density per square mile would be about what it is in India. And yet one sees large areas occupied by no one except herds of cattle that have no market value and which in most sections of the country may not be used for food. These roam over arid expanses underlaid with rock and nibble the scant grasses that grow out of its shallow soil.

Then again we passed the arable tracts, dotted with villages filled with men, women, and children. In places such as these India's masses live. Their houses are crowded closely together. There are no lawns, wide streets, boulevards, or avenues lined with trees. Land in India that produces food is precious. The buildings are of such design and constructed of such materials as the people know how to use and can afford. Most of the village houses are made of mud, and painted with a thin mixture of cow dung, colored earth, and water. Vines grow by the side of their dwellings and climb up over the roof where their fruit is often found. The Bible speaks of grass growing on the housetop and predicts that it will not be able to draw much life out of the dust that accumulates there. But these vines have their roots deep in the earth, and from thence the squash and pumpkins on the roofs of the houses draw their sustenance.

When I came to India it was harvesttime. The rice fields were white and looked as though the yield would be good although the wise farmers said it would be about a "twelve anna" crop. Wielding the scythe is evidently a woman's task in this country as it was in Bible times when Ruth the childless young Moabitess widow went forth to glean after the reapers in the fields of Boaz. Women come to the threshing floor bearing the sheaves on their heads. Here the oxen tread out the grain and

124

when the evening breezes blow it is winnowed as their fathers did millenniums ago. In the midst of the rice fields I saw the little improvised shelters covered with leaves or straw where the proprietor stayed at night keeping watch over his precious crop or piles of grain as did Boaz the night of Ruth's betrothal when she lay at his feet. When I saw this I realized what Isaiah had in mind when he spoke of "a cottage in a vineyard" or a "lodge in a garden of cucumbers."

Manners and customs and the ways of life in India belong to a culture that is old—very old. So much does it differ from the ways of the Western nations that many Occidentals think of the Orientals as being uncultured and as belonging to a primitive civilization. Nothing could be further from the truth. The Indian people are highly civilized and cultured. It is true that their way of living, their customs and manners which are the result of the conditions under which they live are widely diverse from ours. If those who are accustomed to different folkways can lay aside their prejudices and cease to measure the value of other people's possessions by the things they themselves have, they will find much that is beautiful in the simple life of the Easterners. I know their houses look bare without chairs, tables, chests of drawers, divans, couches, refrigerators, and radios. But who decreed that a people has to sit on chairs in order to be civilized, or to eat their food with knives and forks? Or since when and why is the degree of a person's culture based upon whether he eats his peas from the back of his fork like the Englishman or from the other side like the American, or whether he uses his fingers like the Indian or chopsticks like the Chinaman? We hear people say they sit on the floor and eat their food without the use of knife or fork or spoon because they are poor. This is, no doubt, true of many but not of all by any means. How happy the wealthy young couple that sailed with us was when they could take off their shoes and go with bare feet. And how they longed for Indian food served in their native way, without need for implements of serving such as Westerners use.

Entertaining in an Indian home is an art in which the host and hostess express their graciousness fully as well as people of other lands and cultures around the world. Upon arrival at the home, shoes are removed. The guests are seated on a clean sheet or cloth spread along the wall where they sit with feet folded under themselves. Before the meal is served, water, soap, and towel are passed after which come brass plates that are polished till they glitter like Hezekiah's gold. The serving is done with the use of equipment which nature has provided—human fingers. When the meal is finished, water, soap, and towel are again passed. Then everybody is clean—except for what the uninitiated has accumulated on his vest or in his lap. Of course, there are people in India who are not good housekeepers. This is true of all other lands. Many of their quarters are poor—wretchedly poor—and often not clean. But their ways of living fit beautifully into their environment. We hear much these days about raising their standards of living. It should be raised. It is much too low. But just what do we have in mind when we say that? If by that we mean providing facilities that have to do with health and sanitation and cleanliness then we should all be for it. If we have in mind providing ways and means whereby more food and clothing can be made available or housing that contributes to the improvement of the physical, moral, and social well-being, then everyone should certainly be deeply interested and work to the limit of his ability to make these ends possible. If, however, it means imposing upon them our extremely expensive way of life with all its gadgets and contrivances that threaten to become burdensome, then the effort is vain. If it means putting trousers on the men instead of dhotis and dresses on the women instead of saris then we would be doing them less than a favor. Happy are those people, regardless of where they may live, who can take the simple things they have and make them beautiful and be content therewith. These are the ends toward which we should strive. It would be a sad day for the Oriental when solely for the sake of being like other people he would sacrifice what is good and practical, useful and beautiful in his own culture, and substitute traditions from other people who strive madly for a multitude of possessions only to find that they curdle their days and in the end turn into emptiness.

XIII

INDIA'S PEOPLE

Who are the people of India, the charming, colorful multitudes that throng the highways, fill the markets, and jostle each other in the villages and city streets? Ethnologists who have measured the height of the bridge of their noses, the span of their nostrils and have calibrated their skulls to determine whether they are round or oblong or oval tell us that they are Aryans. This means that they are our racial kinsmen and belong to the same general ethnic group as the Europeans and North Americans.

People say they are "well put together" by which they no doubt mean that they are well proportioned and well formed. They are straight, especially the women, who glide along gracefully robed in their saris which set them off with a charm that is not surpassed in any country in the world. From early childhood they have carried their physical burdens on their heads and their grief and sorrows in their hearts. Maybe that's why they stand erect with their shoulders thrown back and their chests forward. The men, like the women, are straight and lithe and agile when not loaded down with disease or with superfluous and useless tissue that becomes burdensome. The corpulent and overfed in India are found in "King's houses," or in the politician's row, or in palaces and among the money-changers. Why their skins are dark and ours are white or less dark, I cannot tell. One can only say that they are a lovely folk, as beautiful and as homely as you and I. Though their surroundings are often far from clean, no one, not even the poorest, they tell us, neglect to have their daily bath. They are kind, courteous, and generous. A retired British engineer who had spent all of his mature life in India assured me that a stranger could travel across the length and breadth of the country, north, south, east, and west without money if he could eat what the people have to offer and sleep in the places that are available.

Separated from their racial kinsmen by wide spaces, hemmed in by the descendants of Shem on the one side and a world of Mongolians on the other, one cannot help wondering where these Aryans come from. Perhaps they are a remnant of Japheth's offspring that did not join the great migration westward when the ambitious building program at Babel collapsed and they were caught in a pocket between their expanding racial competitors on either side—who knows?

Scholars and students who have tried to sift the historical from the legendary and traditional tell us that somewhere across the northern boundary there came into this land of the "Seven Rivers" about two thousand years before Christ, a people, who described themselves in their hymns (the Vedas) as of white complexion with straight, well-bridged noses. This, according to Mr. Ristey, an ethnologist, places them in the Aryan ethnic group. He says further that man's social status in India is determined by the "nasal index," which is to say that his influence and standing varies inversely with the width of his nostrils and the height of the bridge of his nose. By that token, he asserts, one may determine the amount of Aryan (as distinguished from aboriginal) blood that flows in his veins.

The first appearance of these folks seems to have been in the Punjab. In tradition they are spoken of as a pastoral people but their Vedas tell of oxen, sowing and reaping, from which one must conclude that they were also husbandmen and agriculturists.

"O Lord of the field," sings one of their poets, "We will cultivate the field with thee! May the plants be sweet to us. May the rain be full of sweetness; may the field be gracious to us!

Let the oxen work merrily . . . . Let the corn grow with our hymns, let the scythe fall on the ripe grain! Prepare troughs for the drinking animals. Fasten the leathern string and take out the water from this deep and goodly well which never dries up. Refresh the horses, take up the corn stacked in the field and make a cart to carry it easily."

These ancient folks seem to have been a thrifty, happy people. They worshiped "bright gods" which are spoken of as "handsome chinned" by which they may have meant "handsome nosed" since the word meaning "chin" also means nose and the latter is the yardstick by which their racial status is determined.

Today these people are largely idolatrous. This must have been a later development among them for there is nothing in their hymns to indicate that such was their practice when they first settled in the land. Nor is there any mention of caste or enforced widowhood or of child marriage, the bane of India's womanhood. Instead there is reference to a man who married a widow, and to a widow who took a second husband and bore him a son. This, then, is a fleeting glimpse of the ancient people, the progenitors of India's teeming "sun-kissed" millions, a stalwart, fair-skinned, high-nosed race of men with a flair for exhilarating liquor spoken of as Soma. They are found on the land that stretches from the foot of the towering Himalayas to the seas on the East and South and West, though the purity of their stock is now diluted with the blood of the aborigines and others with whom they mixed before caste became frozen and prevented them from crossing its lines.

They were, it seems, deeply concerned with the hereafter, the things that lie in the realm beyond this world. Their yearnings are the same as those of the people of all ages who searched for light on the deepest needs of the soul.

From the earth is the breath and the blood, but whence is the soul? What or who is the one who is never alone, who fans the spheres, who holds the unborn in his hand?

How like the thoughts of Job, the perplexed patriarch of the land of Uz! Out of his affliction he cried:

> Oh that I knew where I might find him!
> That I might come even to his seat.
>
> JOB 23:3

Voices such as these do but express the universal cry of the inner voice of mankind which re-echoes throughout all the ages. The sage of the East who sat in ashes, perhaps about the time of the Aryan invasion of India, found no answer in the mouths of his friends but heard a word of comfort, spoken or unspoken, which came from the Unseen. This he wished might be engraved in a rock with an iron pen for people of all time to read:

> I know that my redeemer liveth, and that he shall stand at the latter day upon the earth: and though after my skin worms destroy this body, yet in my flesh I shall see God.
>
> JOB 19:25, 26

Job received the word but it was one of the descendants of Shem who followed the voice of God which led him westward along the rivers to the "end of the earth" that made possible the realization of the promise. Here under the Star of Bethlehem, "The *Word* became flesh" when in a lowly manger Christ, the highest and fullest revelation of God, was born. He is the answer to the heart yearnings of the race, and the solution to the world's trouble. But this answer has been and now is accepted by pitifully few.

However erroneous the theology of these early invaders may have been and however primitive their concept of God and meager their knowledge, they expressed their thoughts beautifully, almost sublimely, and reveal to us something of their idea of the gods whom they adored:

Many tinted dawn! The immortal daughter of heaven;
    Young, white-robed, come with thy purple steeds;
Follow the path of the dawning the world has been given,
    Follow the path of the dawn the world still needs.

Darkly shining dusk, thy sister has sought her abiding,
    Fear not to trouble her dreams, daughters, you twain of
        the sun.
Dusk and dawn bringing birth! O sisters! your path is unending,
    Dead are the first who have watched, when shall our waking
        be done?

Bright luminous Dawn; rose-red, tinted, radiant rejoicing!
    Show the traveler his road, the cattle their pastures new,
Rouse the beasts of the earth to their truthful, myriad voicing
    Leaders of lightful days, softening the soil with dew.

Wide-expanded Dawn! open the gates of the morning;
    Waken the singing birds! Guide thou the truthful light
To uttermost shades of the shadow for—see you! the dawning
    Is born, white-shining out of the gloom of the night.

The best opinion of those who have made a study of the hymns of the Rig-Veda places their composition as between the years of 2000 and 1400 B.C.—the period which approximates the time involved in the migration of Abraham from Ur to Haran and the Exodus from Egypt. These same hymns which tell us of the Aryan invasion of India tell us also that they found on the soil they then occupied a people far enough advanced in civilization to have towns and well-disciplined armies, weapons, banners, poisoned arrows, and women who wore ornaments of gold. These are called *Dasyas* (Dravidians) or aborigines, a "tawny race who utter fearful yells."

One wonders whether these were the original occupants of India. We hear of rounded mounds which pass for hills underneath which astounding civilizations and cultures lie buried. India is ripe for the spade and rich in material for the archaelogist. Many await the time when the mysteries of these low elevations will be brought into the light of day. But not all the ancient wonders of these people lie covered with the dust of the centuries. There is much that escaped the ravages of time. The highest expression of Hindu art is found in the architecture and

Naples, with Mt. Vesuvius in the background.

A gate in the old Roman wall, Rome, Italy.

Entrance to the Suez Canal.

Ford agency at Aden.

In the hills of North India.

The Taj Mahal, Agra, India.

Kailasa Temple, Ellora, India. It is carved out of solid rock.

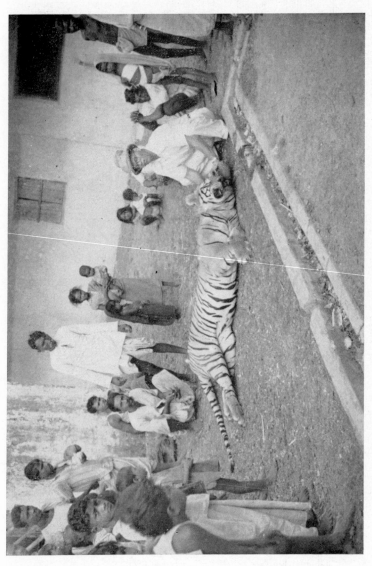

Dr. Jonathan Yoder and his crowd after the tiger hunt.

The general post office, Calcutta, India.

Gardens of the government house, residence of the President of the Republic of India, New Delhi.

design of its temples, its idols, its murals, and other paraphernalia of worship. Among the greatest of these is Kailasa Temple, the great monolith, hewn out of solid rock, located in
Hyderabad State.

For centuries—more than a thousand years—the struggle between the "high-nosed" and the "tawny, reddish with fearful
yells" continued and when finally the ruling dynasty was dispossessed and disposed of, it was not the Dasyas that occupied the
seat of power but the half mystical and half real Naga or Serpent race "an enemy who was flayed of his black skin," whose
history has not yet been disentangled. The trail of these mysteri-
ous people appears again and again in the maze of legend and
now and then crosses the paths of reality only to drop out of
sight and later appear again. In the late fourth century B.C.
when Alexander the Great crossed the borders of India he found
some of the Satrapies held by Serpent Kinglets. Anthropologists
wonder whether these people "flayed of their black skin" may
have been the dreaded Scythians who came down from the
northeast and were contenders with the Aryans for possession of
the land and perhaps infused color into the faces of their "white-
skinned rivals" and deepened that of the "reddish brown" people as they were driven southward and became known to ethnologists as the Aryo-Dravidian synthesis—a fusion similar to that
which took place between the Roman and Germanic elements
in Europe.

How dependable these findings, conjectures, and conclusions
of present-day anthropologists, anthologists, and historians are,
further research in the lore of the ancients will reveal. As of
today the least one can say is that many of the present conclusions do not rest on a very secure foundation and much of reality
is lost in the haze of the past. However a Persian poet, a chron-
icler of the 13th century A.D., satisfied himself by saying that
"fiction which resembles truth is better than the truth which is
dissevered from the imagination." So time will go on and people

will continue dreaming of the races of which the ancient Veda writers sang, and visualizing the life in the cities composed of palaces and streets filled with happy throngs, rich in gold and beautiful women adorned with treasure. Why mar such a picture if nothing better is known with which to supplant it?

Other invasions took place. The wealth of India, its lovely land along the northern border and its fruitful fields, were a temptation to many a marauding host or band of pillagers that swept across the world looking for plunder or for a place to live. Early in the eighth century Muslim Arabs reached the mouth of the Indus River and took over the area known as Sind. Further invasion from that source was blocked until the tenth century when an Afghan Turk, a Muslim, began a series of looting expeditions into the country that for ferocity and cruelty have seldom been equaled. It seemed that the idolatry and caste and other Hindu practices lay heavily upon his conscience and he deemed it not only his duty to carry off whatever wealth he could find but also to convert these heathen or exterminate them. In the twelfth century these followers of Mohammed began to occupy the land and within a score of years they controlled most of North India. After having dispossessed and driven southward many of the occupying tribes they established themselves so thoroughly in what are now the northern provinces that they remain to this day the Mohammedan stronghold of that part of the country.

Another group has sprung up in India's population that amounts to practically a new race, the Anglo-Indian, the offspring of mixed European and Indian marriages or of promiscuous relationships. The group is small, numbering only about 150,000. As late as 1911 they were called Eurasians which was perhaps more nearly correct since they are not purely Anglo-Indian. The origin of the Eurasians dates back more than four hundred years to the time when the Portuguese established themselves on the coast of India near what is now Calcutta. This

134

land was at that time not considered a proper place for European women. It lay miles away and the sea voyage involved a long, tedious journey around the southern point of Africa. In order to establish Portuguese authority in the country the governor encouraged his countrymen to marry Indian women. That the practice might be raised to the level of respectability, only men of approved character were given permission to do so. The women whom they married were as a rule daughters of the leading men of the land. The offspring of these unions became known as Luso-Indians. When later the Portuguese were forced to abandon their Indian holdings this mixed race sank rapidly in the social scale and within two centuries many had reverted to their original status. They are still known as the Goanese, communities of which exist at Goa, Bombay, and at other places on the west coast. In the larger cities, however, they retained their standing and later became amalgamated with the Anglo-Indians.

The beginning of the latter community dates back to approximately 1600 when the East India Company was set up to begin trading operations in what was then a far-off land. This venture naturally brought into the country many soldiers, traders, businessmen, company officials, and employees. Colonies of Englishmen sprang up. Not many English women were willing to undertake the long voyage filled with hardship and seasickness. Consequently the men were encouraged to marry wives from among the Indians. Some of them took unto themselves companions from among the Luso-Indians, others from among the natives. Many children, too, resulted from illegitimate alliances. So important was this practice of intermarriage that the governor at one time offered a stipend of five rupees to mothers for each child born to Englishmen and Indian women. As the years went by the practice decreased because the number of Anglo-Indians increased and new arrivals selected their wives from among them.

For one hundred and eighty-five years this group fared fairly well. They served in the army and filled other positions in the affairs of the company. By 1795 their number had increased so greatly that uprisings were feared. Then they were discharged from their positions and fell "to the status of a downtrodden and proscribed race."

But early in the 19th century a new era once more dawned upon these children of "two peoples." With the introduction of English as the official language of the government and business houses, wide new fields opened unto them. Then came the railroads, the postal system, the telegraph and telephone, all of which presented them with opportunities of service and the day of their prosperity was at hand once more. They became the trainmen, engine drivers, auditors, ticket agents, inspectors, telegraph operators, electricians, postal clerks, policemen, etc. Some were educated in Europe and made their way upward into prominent positions. During my stay in India we were entertained at the home of Judge Bose, a prominent Anglo-Indian who married an American girl from an outstanding family. Since the time of our visit he has been elevated from Chief Justiceship of the Supreme Court of the Middle Provinces to the head of the highest tribunal of justice in the land—Chief Justice of the Supreme Court of India. However, since the withdrawal of the British the glory of this race has again faded. With some exceptions their positions are now being filled by the Indians themselves and their situation is very bad.

The Anglo-Indian today includes in his fold also Indian-born children of pure English families. Among them is the late Bishop W. F. Oldham, the saintly Methodist with whom in company with his lovely Indian-born wife, I crossed the Pampas of the Argentine and the Andes Mountains into Chile in 1920. It was in this group that the Methodist Church made such progress during the preceding century when great numbers were won for Christ under the preaching of such men as William Taylor and others. Many people including the Oldhams, Miss Grace Stephens, and the Westons came from the Anglo-Indian ranks into the fold of the Christian Church and became leaders in its cause.

One more group among the many one finds in India's population is the Parsi, a small community of around 100,000, most of whom live in Bombay. This body, though small in numbers, cannot be overlooked because of the place it holds in Indian life. Long centuries ago their ancestors fled from their Persian home to escape the rule of Islam. They found hospitality and a place to live at Gujarat on the west coast of India. Here they were received by the natives on condition that they respect the Hindu attitude toward the cow, the Hindu marriage traditions and that their women wear the sari. All of these pledges they have faithfully kept. Though they compose a small part of India's large population, they have exerted a tremendous influence upon the cultural and economic life of the country. In the field of business they have been eminently successful. The great Tata steel works at Tatanagur is said to have been founded by a Parsi. They are noted for their integrity and honesty. Their interest in benevolent and educational activities has a religious basis and has greatly benefited the people, the institutions, and the communities where they bestowed their charity. One sees the men on the street with their queer headdress and the women wrapped in their saris. They are a fine-looking race. The men have well-formed bodies, with light olive complexion, aquiline noses, and bright eyes that enable them among other things to see a good business deal. Their women, they say, are good-looking, with fair skins, small hands and feet, beautiful black eyes and long, dark hair. Unlike many of the Oriental women, they do not live in seclusion but come and go in public as do the women of other lands.

These are but a few—very few—of the threads that go to make up the tangled skein of India's population. This is not an attempt to be historical, not even the beginning of it. They are but fleeting glimpses taken from the past into which the author was intrigued when he saw the multitudes of which the Vedas sing, the high-nosed ones, the ones with tawny skins and fearful yells, those flayed of their black skins, and all the other strains that have been interwoven into the life and being of the hosts who occupy this wonderland of the East.

XIV

INDIA'S VILLAGES AND
WAYS OF LIFE

One cannot think of India without taking into account its seven hundred thousand villages and the several hundred million people who live there. In writing about this fascinating land one of its foremost sons, Jawaharalal Nehru, describes it as follows:

When I think of India, I think of many things; broad fields dotted with innumerable small villages, of towns and cities I have visited; the magic of the rainy season which pours life into the dry parched-up land and converts it suddenly into a glistening expanse of beauty and greenery, of great rivers and flowing waters; of the Khyber Pass in all its bleak surroundings; of the southern tip of India; of people, individually and in the mass; and above all, of the Himalayas, snow-capped, or some mountain valley in Kashmir in the spring, covered with new flowers, and with a brook bubbling and gurgling through it.*

How these Indian people love their land so beautifully and richly endowed by nature, so filled with people even though many are steeped in poverty of a depth to which we of the western world are strangers!

It is said that one cannot know India unless he knows its villages where live the overwhelming bulk of its many millions. This is no doubt true. Here exist, without change, the basic institutions of the Hindu way of life. The average village will likely be located in the center of or at the edge of a tract of productive land consisting of several hundred acres on the products

* Nehru, Jawaharalal, *The Discovery of India,* 1946.

of which the fifty to two hundred families will subsist. It will most likely not be located on a paved road although there are many miles of good, well-improved highways in the country. Their water supply is drawn from the community well or more often from a "tank"—a pond outside of the city. Here the people get their drinking water. It is also a place for bathing and furnishes watering facilities for the stock and roving herds of cattle which are often found in the surrounding area. Primitive methods of cultivation and production prevail. The soil is plowed with wooden plows. Pottery is made on the potter's wheel as it was in the day when Jeremiah lived. The juice is extracted from sugar cane by the use of hand mills and the grain is harvested with sickles and threshed beneath the hoofs of oxen.

In a recent book entitled, *India in the New Era,* the author says:

The huts . . . are ramshackle edifices of mud and thatched, with no chimneys or windows. Inside there are dirt floors, rarely tables or chairs, often no beds, and only a few chests and brass pots and pans. Filth and smells are everywhere. Sewage runs along the narrow alleyways. During the rainy season there are noxious pools full of mosquitoes. Garbage and filth litter the village streets.*

A recent traveler describes in a graphic way some of the things he saw while going to and fro across the country where the masses live. He speaks of disease, dirt, and dung which is so commonplace everywhere. In addition to many other things he describes the odors of spice and urine, of garlic and curry powder and dysentery stools, and all the smells of life, decay, and death. No doubt everything exists that is here enumerated and when judged in the light of our culture, much is lacking that we consider essential to the health and physical well-being of mankind. However, not all the things that this observer mentions reflect on the character of India's people. Advancement in cul-

---

* Wallbank, Walter, *India in the New Era,* 1951.

ture does not necessarily depend on the type of household furnishings, culinary equipment, or even the type of houses in which people live. Things like this grow out of the environment within which people live and the materials they have. For example, during my travels in Europe a good friend kept referring to the primitive culture of the American people as compared with that with which he was familiar in his own country. When he was finally asked what elements in our culture he had reference to he referred to the fact that many of the people in the United States still live in houses constructed of lumber. Upon inquiring as to whether he considers the people of Denmark, whose culture antedates that of America by many centuries, as primitive, he replied in the negative and yet most of them live in houses constructed of the same material as are the American homes.

India's climate does not call for large houses, heating plants, or for much clothing. When I think of the simple home of the American pioneers or the fine souls of noble character and high ideals who live in the sod or adobe houses which still dot the desert places or the plains of our own land, I am ready to rise in defense of such as they. Happiness is not necessarily found in elaborate dwellings or furnishings. A number of years ago while riding with one of the residents of that part of the country known as the great plains he pointed to a primitive sod house with sagging earth-covered roof and said, with a touch of honest pride "That's our home." When I entered, I was impressed with its simple appointments. Only half of the floor was covered with flooring. Everything was clean. Out of the ideals of those who dwelt in that humble place there came one of my students who would have been a credit to any institution of learning in the country and who was later a successful teacher in that same community. How well the Saviour knew what was most worth while when He said, "A man's life consisteth not in the abundance of the things which he possesseth." The great apostle affirms that the "kingdom of God is not meat and drink; but righteousness, and peace, and joy in the Holy Ghost."

But the essential needs of the villages and villagers are great. The pools of stagnation need to be drained, sanitation must be provided, attitudes of helplessness repaired, and the things that make for health, better morals, and character must somehow be introduced and put into operation. Missionary agencies have assumed this as part of their task. Communities that have been touched by these influences have risen above those that were beyond the reach of the Christian forces that brought them about. Mission schools have raised the level of literacy, hospitals staffed by well-trained doctors and nurses have struggled with sickness, disease, sanitation, and community welfare with encouraging results. Through the preaching of a Gospel that has to do with a way of life as well as with the things of the spirit, marked advancement has been made in lifting people above their surroundings.

Quoting again from Wallbank, we have the following picture of the changes that are taking place:

The village is changing. Events in the outside world, especially the influence of modern business and city life, are causing it to alter its ancient ways. But the tempo of change is slow. The villagers are the most immobile of all the people; many live and die without traveling as much as fifty miles from the place of their birth. The village is the great fortress of conservatism. Without the benefit of education, only vaguely understanding the slogans of his political leaders, and suspicious of new methods of agriculture, the Indian ryot or peasant dimly appreciates the fact that the standard of living is tragically low, but at the same time he is often the despair of those who try to improve his lot.*

He can, however, tell when he is hungry and he knows the reason why. He knows, too, when he does not have clothing to cover his body or when he is ill. But, no doubt the author of the foregoing quotation is correct when he says that the ordinary villager is suspicious of anything new just as people of other

---

* Wallbank, Walter, *op. cit.*

lands have been when new things were introduced. Historians like to tell the story of the American farmers who at first stubbornly resisted the use of the steel moldboard plow when it came on the market, because they believed that the metal would poison the soil and make it unproductive.

India has millions living in its villages but there are other millions living in her great cities whose lot is on the level of the villager or perhaps below. Here within the shadow of large, beautiful government buildings, banking institutions, hospitals, mills, and factories, they exist in slums. Western civilization has made its impact upon the Orient, which resulted in amazing contacts of which some are good and some evil. One sees businessmen dressed as the Occidentals are, wealthy Indians arrayed in their traditional garb—the dhoti. Side by side with them are the coolies scantily clad and the "holy men" with almost no clothes—sometime none at all. At noon one sees them lying on the sidewalks in the blazing sun. At night there are many hundreds, perhaps thousands, who know no place of rest except such as the entrances of buildings or the pavement afford.

The attraction of a regularly paying job, the failure of crops, hunger, and loss of land draw the poor to the city. Here the village people often fall into unprincipled hands from which they cannot extricate themselves. The housing situation provided for these folks in the city is no better, and often poorer, than that of their village brothers. Inadequate, squalid, and unsanitary as the dwelling places are, they are very expensive. In one of India's largest cities there are blocks of flats crowded with people, living in space poorly ventilated, insufficient lavatory facilities, and no place for the filth and refuse except to dump it outside. One third of the population of these quarters lived in rooms occupied by five persons and eighty thousand lived in rooms occupied by from ten to nineteen people. Beside this, one reads of the "night population" which has no dwelling place at all but belongs to the unnumbered host known as "pavement

143

sleepers." An Indian investigator describes the tragic situation in the following terms:

In one room of the second floor of a *chawl* (rooming house) measuring fifty by twelve feet, I found six families living . . . . On inquiry, I ascertained that the actual number of adults and children in this room was thirty. . . . Three of the six [women] were shortly expecting to be delivered. . . . When I questioned the nurse who accompanied me as to how she would arrange for privacy in this room, I was shown a small space four by three feet which was usually screened off for this purpose. The atmosphere of that room, at night, filled with smoke from the six ovens and other impurities would certainly handicap any woman with an infant both before and after delivery.

In one of those places it is said that 180,000 people have access to only 460 faucets for their water supply. Open sewage, garbage, filth, and flies abound everywhere, and yet rents are exorbitantly high when compared with the laborers' income. To all the problems which this group faces, there must be added the inequality in the number between the sexes. Usually the women outnumber the men, often as much as two to one. This leads to immorality which, together with a lack of recreational facilities and squalor of surroundings, leads to other vices and degrading practices. It is claimed that the situation of the urban worker is more desperate and debasing than that of the villager.*

Some will say that these conditions are the product of the people: that they have created the conditions under which they live. Others will say that the people are shiftless and care for nothing better. Some lay the blame on the exploitation of the poor by the rich; others have tried to saddle it upon the British. Still others ascribe it to their religion with its caste and other practices which they say take no account of morals or character. Perhaps all these factors and more have contributed to the situation which is now difficult to overcome. We know that India's leaders and many among the masses long for something better but find the way strewn with difficulties and problems that are hard to overcome.

---

* Rao, B. Shiva, *The Industrial Worker in India*, 1939.

What are the needs of the average villager or urban laborer? The economist and social worker will state these in a few words —income, food, housing. Not too many years ago the Indian counted his income in pice and annas. Today he computes it in rupees, but he is not better off now than he was before on account of the higher cost of living. The results of this are improper diet, undernourishment, poor health, reduced physical stamina and a low life expectancy. Every year nearly six million deaths result from preventable diseases. Malaria alone takes a toll of one million lives annually. Tuberculosis, typhoid, cholera, leprosy, and venereal diseases also claim a heavy share of human life. The factors that contribute to this terrible toll are for the most part controllable—contaminated water, lack of sanitation, poor housing, flies and mosquitoes, and malnutrition. Until these major diseases are checked the ravages upon life will continue. Sixty-five per cent of its people die before they are thirty, and every child that is born has only an even chance of growing to maturity. Life expectancy in India is twenty-six years. Out of every 100,000 babies born alive only one half live to be over five years.

To date public health facilities are entirely inadequate to serve the needs of all classes. Those who are in a position to know say that in 1941 there was one doctor available for 6,000 people, one nurse for every 43,000, one dentist for every 300,000. Along with this lack of professional help there are the problems that must be attributed to ignorance and superstition. In 1941 only 12.5 per cent of the population was literate in its own language, and a much smaller percentage in the English language. The rate, however, is much higher in the Christian group and in the communities touched by Christian schools. The need of the Indian village people and the laborers crowded into the tenements of the cities presents a sad picture. It should touch the heart of all who find themselves more favorably situated and who are in a position to bring about reforms that will make for a more equitable distribution of resources available for the betterment of the people as a whole. When, however, anyone undertakes any project that involves a change of habits and folkways he soon learns how deeply they are rooted into the life of the people regardless of what race and nationality they are, whether they live in Boston or Philadelphia of the U.S.A. or in Calcutta or Bombay.

The problems of India, however, are not entirely rooted in those that grow out of land and food distribution nor those that grow out of labor and employment conditions. The Indian people are deeply religious. This is a tremendously strong factor in the entire situation. Statisticians tell us that the Hindu community includes about 65 per cent of the population within the embrace of its faith. Its doctrines affect the social status of its followers, and determine the people with whom they can associate, the occupations in which they may engage, and the food they may eat. Even marriage is limited by religious status. Practically all these restrictions and limitations upon life are the result of caste which has been defined as follows:

The cast system, Wallbank says, is the classification of all individuals, according to the occupation they traditionally follow, the circle within which they must marry, and the group with whom they may mingle socially.

Status is not a matter of choosing. It is acquired through birth, and it is not transferable. Each caste is an exclusive group. Each one also has its own regulations and traditions which have to do not only with marriage, occupation, and the broader aspects of human life and interrelationships but also with such fine details as table practices, table companions, table servants, etc. To violate the dictates of caste is serious and places the offender in difficult relationship with his own group and does not improve his standing with any of those outside his faith.

Caste has been outlawed, they say, since the British are gone and the Indians have taken over, but old traditions die hard and it will be interesting to see how well they will handle the problem and pull themselves out of the shackles that bind them. It will also be interesting to discover whether new divisions based on wealth, education, etc., will spring up as they did in other lands and become as arrogant and almost as binding as those of which the Indians are trying to rid themselves.

In contrast with the meditative and contemplative Hinduism with its polytheism, taboos, and conservatism, stands monotheistic Mohammedanism, aggressive, almost fanatical, dynamic, and free from the divisions and limitations which caste imposes upon the Hindu. Regulations regarding the eating of meat do not bother the followers of Mohammed, but to the Hindu this is forbidden and the sacred cow must not be killed under any circumstances. The Hindu has no compunction of conscience against taking interest on his money while the Moslem does. The Hindu also took up earlier with western education and thus won for himself positions in government and a recognized place in the professions. This, together with the Muslims' aversion to money lending, gave the Hindus the advantage and they came to be a dominant factor in business, landownership, banking, etc. This in part is responsible, so authorities say, for the ill feeling between the two groups in past decades. The Mohammedan group embraces about 24 per cent of India's population, the majority of whom were of Hindu origin. Following the Muslim invasion a large number of Hindus accepted this new religion, some of them voluntarily, others to escape death.

It has already been mentioned that Hinduism is more than a mere faith—it is a way of living that reaches into every area of a person's life. This is true also of Mohammedanism. In contrast with the Hindu caste system it includes such tenets as the equality of man. It rejects child marriage but accepts polygamy. These and other items of faith and practice place a wide gulf between these two major religious groups. During the years these rivalries have become aggravated and the chasm has wid-

147

ened until the flood of hatred broke out in the violence that followed Indian Independence, including riots, loss of life, migrations, and hardship that cannot be described.

At the head of the list of the smaller religious groups stands the Christian Church with more than six million believers. This is now the third largest group in India. It is largely the result of the modern Christian missionary effort which sprang up less than two centuries ago. In addition to the spreading of the Gospel this movement concerned itself also with the problem of education, the production of Christian literature in the languages of the people, and with health and sanitation. Printing presses have been set up from which a stream of literature has come. Hospitals and medical service have followed the missionaries to remote places within the country. Grade and high schools and colleges have made a large contribution to the educational uplift of the people. Literacy in the Christian communities is much above that of the population as a whole. It is said that Christianity has drawn most of its converts from the lower castes including the untouchables. However, these outcastes and low caste people when brought into contact with the power of the Gospel have risen above their surroundings and rank to be among the choicest of India's millions.

Outstanding among the minority religious groups of India are the Parsis and the Sikhs. The former were originally followers of Zoroaster. In size the group is small, numbering about one hundred thousand. Their original home was in Persia. The Sikhs are said to be neither a "race, a nationality, nor a caste" but a religion. They number about six million members. They are not idolatrous nor do they recognize caste and they are opposed to Brahmanism. They fought the persecuting Muslim during the time of the early invasions and won high renown for their military prowess. They early became the soldiers of India and built up a strong militant brotherhood. When conquered by the British they served in the armies of the crown and became

148

famous for their heroic and soldierly qualities. As policemen they hold the place in the Oriental possessions of the British that the Irish hold in the nations of the West.

India—land of contrasts—the lovely and the unlovely side by side—what a world of humanity you are! When touched by the magic hand of Divine Grace beauty has sprung from the dust and the glory of the Lord has fallen from on high upon the land and the people who have chosen to walk in the steps of the Man of Galilee.

11

XV

THE MENNONITE CHURCH IN INDIA

November 22, 1949, marked the fiftieth anniversary of the founding of the American Mennonite Mission in India. A half century before that a small party of Americans consisting of J. A. Ressler and Dr. and Mrs. W. B. Page arrived at Dhamtari in the Central Provinces, now Madhya Pradesh. They made their tedious trip from Raipur by oxcart, and pulled into a field at the edge of a mango grove where they pitched their tent and made preparations to camp for the night. They had been led into a hungry land by those who had gone before with food and clothing to relieve the suffering, destitute people. Much as such provisions and medicines were needed, the people of America felt that such was not enough. Had not the Master who concerned Himself greatly with the physical needs of man also ministered to the needs of the soul as well as to those of the body?

When these strangers arrived, the country was in the midst of famine. The highways, streets, and markets were filled with hungry, starving, sick, diseased, crippled, and despairing people. There were no spiritual kinsmen nor friendly faces of acquaintances to greet the strangers and offer them the hospitality to which they were accustomed. Only the "shadows" of the emaciated, wide-eyed multitude hovered around these white-skinned folks from a foreign land who had come into their midst. They wondered, no doubt, who these peculiar people were that seemed so strangely appareled and spoke in a tongue that none of them knew. What feelings must have been stirred in the bosom of these newcomers when they for the first time saw the village that was to become their home and the people dying with hunger who would be their townsmen, their neighbors, and brethren in the faith!

What a change time and patient toil has wrought during the fifty years since that eventful day! Now there are those who are clothed and fed and housed and enjoy the things of the Spirit that the Gospel has to offer. Men and women who were then hungry orphans—often on the point of starvation—are now clean, keen-minded and healthy. Some of them are ministers of the Gospel, others are teachers, compounders, nurses, Bible women, evangelists, farmers, and businessmen whose lives, having been transformed by Divine Grace, would be a credit to any Christian community. There are churches and schools filled with happy, playing children who enjoy the love and affection of parents whose nature has been renewed and whose spirit has been tempered through the power of a loving God.

The morning of the day which marked the anniversary of the arrival of the first missionaries broke beautifully as the mornings of the winter season of India do. Hard by the place where the original travelers camped on their arrival when they first came, a platform was erected for the speakers of the occasion and an awning was raised to cover the gathering crowds. On the compounds surrounding the dwellings of the missionaries the visiting workers had put up the tents which were to be their home during this sojourn. Members from the surrounding congregations were encamped by their oxcarts or were strewn across the field where the meetings were to be held. This was a great day for them and their children. Meetings like this which are so frequent among us as to become almost commonplace and uninteresting are new in other lands and are looked forward to with much anticipation.

At the appointed hour people began to gather on the church grounds. They formed in marching order, with the members of each congregation together under its own banner which contained a verse of Scripture as its motto. With colors afloat the procession marched to the camp site singing the beautiful songs of their native tongue. The road was lined with people who must have been impressed when they realized how many Christians lived among them and saw the spirit that marked the decorum of the group. About noon of the first day some twenty Christian women from the leper home at Shantipur five miles away came on the grounds and sat a short distance apart from the tent. They had walked all the dusty miles, some with diseased feet and leprous sores, in order to be allowed the privilege of listening in on the meetings, though the isolation forced upon them by their physical condition forbade them to mingle with their brothers and sisters in the faith.

For two days the meeting proceeded according to schedule. Indians as well as missionaries participated in the service. The people, including some Americans, sat on the straw bedded earth in accordance with the custom of the country, and maintained an attitude of interest and quietness that would be commendable in a similar service in any community. Delegates from other missions were present and an excellent program was rendered in which representatives of the Indian Church and missionaries participated. The meeting reached its climax at the closing session held in the evening of the second day. At that time the different types of service offered by the mission were re-enacted by groups of people present. There were scenes of village evangelistic meetings, hospital scenes, schoolroom activities, and leper treatments, to acquaint the people with the work that is being carried on by the mission. The outstanding number on the program was put on the members of the Mangal Tarai community who belonged to the untainted leper colony. Those who witnessed the scene will long remember the enthusiasm of the little boy who brought his candle to the flame of the "great light" and went away singing as he carried it, in his imagination, to "all the world."

What a joy it was to see the results of these years of work! Fifty years ago this community was completely shrouded in pagan darkness. The message of the love of God and redemption through Jesus Christ had never been heard. It was a place where sin brooded over the masses, where ignorance and superstition abounded, where there was no balm for diseased bodies nor sin-sick souls. Now, after so short a time there was a multitude present that bore the marks of the grace of God, intelligent, capable and interested in things divine. What means of philanthropy, what acts of legislation, what science or philosophy, what power save the power of God could bring about such a transformation!

When people question what motive could prompt men and women to separate themselves from the pleasant associations of their native haunts and endure inconveniences, often disappointments, and seemingly fruitless toil, in order to persuade men to accept a mode of thought and way of life to which they have been alien, there is but one answer—"The love of Christ constraineth us." The great apostle justifies this attitude on the ground of his conviction that all must "appear before the judgment seat of Christ; that every one may receive the things done in his body." "Knowing therefore the terror of the Lord, we persuade men . . . ," he says. Therefore, "whether we be beside ourselves . . . or whether we be sober, it is for your cause." Knowing then these things, that which may seem to many irrational becomes the most logical thing for the Christian to do.

Ever since the days of the Apostle Paul, men and women have followed in his footsteps and have gone to far lands to live and labor among strange people whose ideologies, faiths, and ways of life are as widely different from their own as is the evening from the morning. They are the bearers of divine love, "stewards of the manifold grace of God," bearing their treasures in earthen vessels as Christ Himself did, that nations may learn to know Him whom to know is life eternal.

When one looks at the work from the short range of a single lifetime, the results may seem meager, and when set up against the cost in energy and life and other resources, the expenditure may seem unjustifiable. But when measured in terms of what has happened since first these saints of God began to move in the spirit of Him who gave them their commission, more than nineteen centuries ago, we are forced to the conclusion that no group more important than they has ever trodden the earth. In faraway lands and islands of the sea, in cities and countryside as well as in deserts remote, often among hostile people and in the midst of unfriendly surroundings they have gone to reclaim by grace divine the human wreckage of the ages. Out of their labors have risen souls created anew, transformed into the image of God, who became a blessing in their day and for all time. You ask them why all this sacrifice, self-denial, and toil and the answer will be the same, "The love of Christ constraineth us!"

When the missionaries first arrived at Dhamtari the question of what to do next and where to begin was decided for them. The need was pressing. Hungry, starving people had to be fed. Orphans needed to be taken care of, the sick had to be ministered unto. They abounded on every hand. For more than a year after the work in that area began their time was occupied with feeding the hungry and trying to alleviate the suffering occasioned by the shortage of food. During this period they undertook to supply government rations to around thirty thousand government employees and famine victims in some thirty-five to forty villages surrounding Dhamtari. As soon as it became possible their efforts were shifted from the feeding program to that of caring for the homeless children. A plot of ground consisting of some nine acres was secured on which the mission schools, orphanage, church, and mission homes now stand. It is known as *Sundarganj,* "Beautiful Treasure," which it indeed was and now is. Since then it has been the home or the headquarters of the mission and church.

The work grew. The first group of sixteen orphans which came from Raipur increased and at one time reached the total of more than six hundred. Out of this number came some of the present leaders of the church—M. Sukhlal, Mukut Bhelwa, and Parsadi. The second of these told his congregation at Ghatula, on the occasion of my visit, that the Mennonite Board of Missions and Charities was the only father and mother he ever knew. It gave him food and clothing and shelter when he was a motherless, starving child. It gave him what learning he has and above all it taught him the way of life through its missionaries and teachers. He is now a minister of the Gospel and has a lovely family, all of whom have a college or nursing education and are engaged in their respective fields as Christians who strive to do their work in the name and spirit of the Lord.

Since that day many things have happened. New missionaries have been added to the original number. They came as doctors, nurses, teachers, and ministers. All of them were evangelists and preached the unsearchable riches of Christ Jesus. Children were born and grew to maturity among these alien people whom they loved as their own, some died and lie buried on India's hills and plains. Churches, schools, and hospitals came into existence and grew into prosperous institutions supplying the need of the communities which they are designed to serve.

The primary interest of the Mennonite church in India, as in all its missionary endeavor, is spiritual. It has to do with the preaching of the Gospel, the reclaiming the lost, and bringing into a united fellowship those who believe. This is the highest duty of the Christian church. But it is aware of other human needs which were also the concern of Jesus and His followers. Realizing this the mission has busied itself with ministering to the physical, economic, intellectual, and moral needs of the people for whom it is responsible. Since the work had its beginning in the famine of 1897, food, clothing, and medical needs were pressingly imposed upon the missionaries. Out of this grew the present General Hospital which is located on the outskirts of the city of Dhamtari, a large Leper Home at Shantipur, and the roadside clinics for the benefit of those who cannot take advantage of the services offered at the Leper Home. Beside this there are clinical facilities at practically all the stations.

From the earliest beginnings of the mission program the church realized that a live and effective church would have to be literate. In the absence of schools operated by the community the missionaries wisely proceeded to provide such facilities themselves. At practically all the stations schools are operated for the village children.

But this is not all. "The poor have the gospel preached to them." Organized congregations have sprung up in a half score of places, practically all staffed with Indian pastors. In addition to this there are many preaching points where the Word is being proclaimed more or less regularly. The missionaries, being relieved from pastoral responsibility, are free to engage in village evangelization during the part of the year when weather conditions make it possible.

The work of the Mennonite church is no longer confined to the Central Provinces. Recently a new district was opened in Bihar Province, a section north and west of Calcutta. A number of families are now established here. Suitable sites have been located as centers from which the work is to be carried on. The people of this area seem to be responsive to the teachings of the Gospel and the outlook for the future is promising.

What the years hold for India in the next half century, no one but God alone can know. What lands and people will survive the world upheaval, or who that was present at the celebration of the fiftieth anniversary will be present fifty years hence when the centennial mark is reached, no one can predict. But we do know the Saviour's promise: "Lo, I am with you alway, even unto the end of the world." With such a pledge, we dare not but face the future with hope even though the way is not

156

always clear and the difficulties are without number. The manifestations of the grace of God are always impressive and wherever people accept it the regenerating work of the Spirit follows. The many who have been lifted above their surroundings through their knowledge of the Word and have lived victoriously over corruption and sin are witness to the fact that the Word has not been preached in vain. With such as they the church of India will be built, and to them we shall look for a testimony that will bring within the gates of righteousness, into the fold of the Lord, the multitudes that are now scattered over the hills and plains throughout the jungles of that beautiful land.

XVI

FROM STATION
TO STATION

I received my first view of the Dhamtari area on a moonlight night in late October. After a long train ride of a night and a day we arrived at Raipur where we were met by Dr. and Mrs. J. G. Yoder and Mrs. George Beare. They had our evening meal ordered at a restaurant near the railway station. The setting of this eating house brought up memories of the places where I ate years ago when we lived on the frontier in the Great American Desert in the State of Washington. Why these visions should come out of the past at a place half a world away is more than I can tell. Certainly the people are not the same. Instead of the booted, high heeled, and spurred men arrayed in goatskin chaps, silk mufflers, and ten-gallon hats, there were those clad in dhotis with turbaned heads and bare feet. In that respect there was not much similarity except that the deeply tanned faces of the plainsmen were not much less dark than the skins of those who hung around this Indian restaurant. Perhaps it was the simplicity of the surroundings, the absence of table linen, the bare walls, the meager furnishings and tableware, the rubbish-littered streets, and the hungry dogs that haunted the place looking for scraps of food that escaped the vigilance of the beggars who vied with them for anything that might be cast away. It may be, too, that it was the clear light of the full moon and the myriads of stars in an unclouded sky, free from the hazy film that dims their light in lands where the humidity is always high. Perhaps, too, the smell of the dusty roads, and what in our land would be considered the flimsy and primitive structures along the streets and highways had something to do with my feelings. But the meal was good. Boiled eggs, unless they are overripe, cannot be spoiled by cooking.

BALODGAHAN

The moonlight ride along the highway from Raipur brought us to Balodgahan to the home of Mr. and Mrs. George Beare who had then spent more than a score of years in the country as missionaries. My bed, covered with mosquito netting securely tucked in on all sides, stood on the wide veranda. This gave me some feeling of security. I had heard so many stories of snakes that I could not resist the impulse to explore the length of the mattress and all the folds of the covers to assure myself that none had intruded into the space set apart for me, and having satisfied myself, I bade the world good night.

The next morning I was awake early and listened to the village noises—the cackling of the geese which one of the inmates of the widows' home was shepherding, the song of the birds, and the barking of dogs. I saw the silent forms of women, sari-clad, gliding across the compound. I heard the children on their way to school and saw the women bearing their sickles going to the little field of rice for it was harvest time. Everything seemed so new. Only once that I can recall did I experience such a sensation. It was years ago when I awoke for the first time in the stillness of a timeless land, the desert, far from the haunts of men. After an Indian breakfast prepared by an efficient Indian cook and served by an Indian maid—I think it was a maid, it might have been a man—we drove to Dhamtari to get whatever mail had accumulated at that place and made plans for the next few days of my stay in the community.

Balodgahan is more than a mission station. The entire village together with a valuable tract of tillable land was, at the time of my visit, owned and governed by the mission. The missionary who was then in charge of the station was also the

Malguzar of the community which occupied the land and village buildings. Since then all such holdings have been officially abolished and their control has been taken over by the state.

It was at this place where I first met the missionaries as a group. Some business matters brought together the men who are located in the area, and they in turn brought their wives and children and the single women came also. It was a happy meeting and afforded all of us a pleasant afternoon with business interspersed with visiting and the inevitable tea which is always served wherever the flag of England floats.

Here at this place I saw my first tragedy. The night of my arrival was cool and an old lady who lived in a corner of the compound set a tub of smoldering charcoal under her bed to keep herself warm. While she slept the covers slipped into the fire and set the bed aflame. She was badly burned and died at the hospital the next morning. During the following day her body, covered with a sheet, lay on a bed in the shade of a tree, while the yards of red tape necessary in order to secure a burial permit, were being unwound. Finally, about dark, the remains were consigned to mother earth and the spirit was committed to the care of a kind and merciful heavenly Father.

The congregation at this place consists of some three hundred fifty members. The Christian community which includes adults and children numbers nearly six hundred. An Indian pastor, Brother Sukhlal, has charge of the church and is a conscientious shepherd of his flock. On a Sunday morning I preached to this interesting and inspiring group of believers and their families. After the preaching service several members who had been excommunicated previously were reinstated into the fellowship of the church.

DHAMTARI

My next visit took me to Dhamtari. Here is located the mother church of the Mennonites in India. On the first Sunday afternoon of my stay in this area I had the privilege of preaching at an English service held once per month in the late afternoon. What an inspiration it was to speak to this large number of people in my own language! The audience consisted of teachers, businessmen, farmers, compounders, nurses, and missionaries as well as those who are landless and poor. During the long years of my ministry I have never spoken to a more responsive and appreciative audience. They were my brothers and sisters in the Lord, intelligent, clean, and saved by the same Saviour that you and I know. They are deeply interested in the work of the church. Mrs. Samida, wife of the principal of the high school, served as chorister. She led the congregation in singing the songs that we sing here at home. A girls' chorus from the high school directed by Verna Burkholder Troyer also took part in the service. I will likely forget some of the experiences I had in India—I have already—but the memory of these vesper services will remain with me.

The congregation at this place consists of more than five hundred members. The church building is large and substantial. John Haider who came to the Christian faith from Mohammedanism is the pastor. He is able and well qualified for the work. Here again the church is removed from the city and stands on a tract of land where the schools are and where the missionaries and many of the teachers live. The buildings are located in a lovely setting in the midst of trees, shrubs, and flowers, such as India's climate makes possible.

SHANTIPUR

My next visit took me to Shantipur which literally means a city of peace. The congregation at this place is composed largely of patients and residents of the Leper Home, and is in charge of an Indian pastor. We arrived at the church rather early and saw the lepers filing in quietly and reverently to take their place for worship. In my travels in India I nowhere saw a more impressive audience than here among these poor folks. Long before the days of Moses people afflicted with the disease from which these people suffer were doomed to live apart from the rest of humanity. While they are denied much that others may enjoy they have other compensations that make up for what their fate as lepers deprives them of.

In the evening, accompanied by Arnold Deitzel, I enjoyed the first entertainment in an Indian home. The pastor of the congregation, Brother O. P. Ram, was not only host, but also the one who prepared and served the food. His wife was at the hospital where she had undergone surgery, hence he was in charge of everything, and everything was well done.

The church at Sankra was at one time one of the larger ones, although at present its membership is considerably reduced. It is from this station that the Roadside Leper Clinics were operated at the time of my visit. This place also maintains a school with two teachers as well as a clinic and dispensary in charge of a trained compounder. A very active evangelist is located here and does excellent work in village visitation and evangelization. The one regret that I have in connection with this congregation is that my schedule did not make it possible for me to be present for any of the worship services.

DONDI

Early one morning before the day dawned, Paul Miller accompanied by his family and myself drove away from the Sankra mission home on our way to Dondi, one of the newer churches, where John Friesens at that time lived. This station is beautifully located in a hilly section of the country, parts of which are densely covered with timber. A heavy caliber rifle rested on the seat between the driver and myself. In the early part of the day deer and other animals that are late in returning to the security of their retreats often become an easy prey for the hunter. We met up with several such, but they were too cunning and shrewd for us and before we got within range they had made their way to cover.

The Dondi church has a membership of thirty-five. During

my stay they observed their Thanksgiving service. A small but interesting crowd of people was present. The deacon of this congregation, Brother Sadhuram, and his wife are lovely folks. One evening during my visit the congregation gathered under the open sky for a meal together. We ate under the light of the stars and concluded our fellowship with a brief worship service after the meal was finished. One could not help but feel that these people, though in many ways widely separated from the westerners, had caught the spirit of the same Lord whom we also know. This church and home stand apart from the village as do the missionary establishments at all or nearly all the other stations. One wonders why this is and whether it may help to foster a feeling of segregation on the part of the Indian people, although I know that those who promoted such a policy did what in their opinion was best.

Mangal Tarai

From Dondi we returned to Dhamtari where I spent a few days in the homes of Mr. and Mrs. S. M. King and Mr. and Mrs. Edwin I. Weaver. Later I went to Mangal Tarai with Ralph Smucker to visit the colony of symptom-free lepers. This work was started by the late George Lapp who spent a number of years here in an attempt to build up the community. When we arrived we found a group of people waiting for us at the entrance of their little village. After a brief speech of welcome and a brief response I was decorated with a wreath of marigolds as a token of their friendship and good will. As a colonizing project this undertaking has not prospered greatly. At present there are a number of Christian families located here. A small school is maintained for the children of the community. Church services are held in the schoolhouse when a minister is available. We returned to the Paul Miller home in the evening in time for a roast peafowl dinner.

Ghatula

Some miles away, separated from the Dhamtari area by a

sizable river and miles of jungle road is the Ghatula station. The mission compound contains the residence of the missionaries, the church, the clinic, and the school. There is no bridge across the river—only a causeway which during the rainy season is usually so damaged that it is not usable until it has been repaired. Consequently at such times the stream has to be forded. This is an undertaking which is not without its perils. En route to Ghatula neither the causeway nor the river could be crossed by an automobile. Hence coolies carried my baggage on their heads while I removed my shoes and waded the forty or so rods to the opposite shore where Weyburn Groff and family were waiting for me. Scattered across the country are government buildings furnished and equipped for the use of officials whose duties take them hither and yon from time to time. When not occupied these houses are available also for other travelers. They are known as Dak bungalows. It was at one of these places that we stopped for lunch. It was situated on a high eminence overlooking a beautiful lake in the midst of a lovely jungle. Here with the help of an Indian woman our party finally succeeded in getting a fire kindled to brew some tea for our evening meal. Long before we arrived at Ghatula night descended upon us and we enjoyed the evening sounds of the forest as we followed the road to our destination.

The people of each country have their own way of welcoming strangers. Here as well as at other places the people had planned a reception. Owing to the lateness of the hour most of the ceremonies had to be abandoned. We were escorted to our bungalow with drums beating and music from some of their native instruments. That was the first and only time that I was met by a band. The next morning an Indian brother and his wife came and performed the ceremony of decorating their guest with the traditional wreath of marigolds.

Ghatula is located among low mountains. They are always impressive and I can well see why the Psalmist found comfort in lifting up his "eyes unto the hills." Amid a cluster of Indian homes is located the mission compound, with its church, dispensary, school, and residences for the missionaries. At one time the Bible School was located at this place but it has since been abandoned and the building is now used for other purposes. The bungalows are set in the midst of palm trees, shrubs, and flowers —a beautiful setting. Each morning we ate our breakfast on the open veranda which made one feel the goodness of the out-of-doors and gave us the warmth of the morning sun.

The work at this place was then in charge of Weyburn and Thelma Groff. The local congregation was in the care of Brother Mukut Bhelwa, one of the orphans that was salvaged from the famine in the beginning of our work in India. The membership of this church numbers around one hundred. I happened to arrive here at the time of their annual Thanksgiving services and had the opportunity of speaking to them through an interpreter, which mode of communication is never very satisfactory. I saw them bring their offerings of rice, squash, chickens, and whatever else they had to offer and lay them down on the floor in front of the pulpit. After the service the produce and other materials were sold to the public at an auction sale. I presume auctioneers are found in every land on the globe and their practices and tactics are everywhere similar. During the morning service a crippled old lady hobbled into the church on her haunches and laid her gift alongside that which others had brought. Moved with pity, I bought a chicken at the sale and gave it to her. When later in the day I visited her home I found the yard full of poultry and then wondered whether my charity was wisely bestowed—she evidently did not need a chicken. The auctioneer needed a shirt, I was told, so I bought the only one that was offered for sale and gave it to him. I hope he was not overstocked with similar garments.

When we arrived at the church for the evening service, we felt a tenseness among the worshipers. Upon inquiry, we were informed that they had found a cobra about four feet long which had taken possession of the pulpit and was lying along the wall behind the chairs. The pastor with the help of some of the members succeeded in bringing about her demise so that when we arrived only the blotch of blood was left.

MOHADI

After a few days at this place we were on the road again to Mohadi which is located on a wide plain not far from the edge of an extensive forest. The congregation at this place numbers around fifty members. Wilbur Hostetler and wife are in charge of this work. Sunday morning worship was held in a nice little church building. One evening we accompanied Mrs. Hostetler to a home in the village where she was called to minister to a sick baby. When a person sees the conditions under which some of these children live and the way their food is prepared he can understand why they are bothered with colic and kindred ailments and why they do not get along well.

The mission is situated on a large compound. Villages are scattered over the plain and throughout the jungle. Some of the members live in the more remote places along the highway or in the forest. Some of these scattered people seem devoted to their faith even though they are not able to attend services regularly and live among those who are not in sympathy with their religion. The mission home stands in the midst of a large compound enclosed with a substantial brick wall about six feet high. The line of small cabins which was designed as quarters for servants and employees reminded me somewhat of the pictures of Southern plantations in ante bellum days. This project evidently did not develop in accordance with the original plan and some of these small huts are now used by employees and members of the church, while others are vacant.

TO DHAMTARI FOR THE ANNIVERSARY

From here my itinerary took me back to Dhamtari for the

anniversary celebration. I also got a glimpse of what it means to get ready to attend such a meeting. The Hostetler oxcart was loaded with bedding, food, tents, cooking equipment, baggage, and even some furniture such as cots and camp chairs. A day or so before our departure several employees set off with the outfit. They were presumed to have the tent set up and everything in order by the time the missionary family arrived. We reached the place after an interesting trip through the forest. While crossing the river our jeep got flooded and in the process of pulling it out, the gears stuck. This left some of us wondering whether we would need to make the rest of the trip on foot. The missionary, however, was equal to the occasion and got the trouble fixed. A band of coolies pulled the jeep out of the mire and set it on its way.

When we arrived at Dhamtari we found everything in order. The beds were set up and the floor was carpeted with clean rice straw. The family was soon located for the duration of the meeting and the living quarters took on something of the air of an outing. The place looked so inviting that I was rather sorry to move into the good room at Dr. Yoder's home. When during the night the mosquitoes went into action I concluded that my sleeping quarters were far better suited to my needs than a tent would have been and was profoundly thankful for the thoughtfulness and consideration of my good friends who knew better than I how to plan for my welfare.

DRUG

North and west of the Dhamtari area on the main line of the Bombay-Calcutta Railway is located the city of Drug where one of our churches is situated in a field on the outskirts of the municipality. I arrived there in early December when the Royal Bauers were in the process of being oriented into the life and ways of India. This station came to us from the Methodists. It is located in a beautiful setting a little off the main highway leading to town. The church building is a substantial brick structure, well designed and well adapted to the India situation. There are no comfortable church benches to afford drowsy members a dozing place during the service. In fact, there are no benches at all unless they have been added since my visit. The worshipers sit on the floor in accordance with the custom of the country. The congregation consists of one hundred thirty members and is in charge of Brother Sonwani, an Indian pastor in whose home we were entertained at tea. In addition to the churches I visited, there are a number of preaching places scattered throughout the Dhamtari area, where regular services are held.

On to Bihar

North and west of Calcutta in the Bihar area a new field has been opened within the last decade. This work is located in a beautiful section of the country. There are mountains in view from some of the stations and large jungles and rice fields adorn the landscape. Herds of cattle roam over the open areas as they do in other parts of the land. At the time of my visit there were three missionary families in this section—Milton Vogts, Henry Beckers, and John Beachys. The work is small but encouraging. After having spent a few days in Calcutta, Henry Becker and I traveled by train to Latehar where we arrived after a long-drawn-out wait at a division point along the railway. After what seemed an endless half day of waiting, the train finally arrived and took us to our destination where we were met by Gladys Becker and her three children who took us to their home where we sat down to a delicious supper and later slept in a comfortable bed. The work here is almost entirely evangelistic. Mrs. Becker, a registered nurse, maintains a small dispensary where people are given such service as she is able to render. A municipal hospital is located in the town close by. An Indian medical man is in charge and his service is said to be quite satisfactory.

One moonlight evening we drove to a near-by village where the rice was stacked and people were making preparations to thresh. Here a service was held by the Beckers assisted by several Indian Christians. The people were attentive—a few even ventured to ask questions. On Sunday we attended church at Chandwa where the Vogts are in charge. This happened to be an unusual occasion. After the sermon there was a betrothal ceremony. A young man and woman who had perhaps not spoken to each other previously stood before the pulpit while Brother Vogt spoke to them in a language which I did not understand. Judging from the effect upon the young couple and their friends who were present, it was effective and helpful. Some months later the wedding was to take place and a new family was to be sent on its way. The next day a workers' meeting was held in one of the homes. All the members of the church were together in a small house where we enjoyed a blessed time of fellowship in the things of God. At noon the meal was served on the veranda and the afternoon was spent in looking over the site where a new station was to be opened. The next morning we started for Rangadih where the United Missionary Church has a mission. The trip took us through beautiful country. The forest-covered mountains are always alluring but here in India they seem all the more charming, perhaps because of the arid stretches that are so brown and drab during the dry season of the year.

At Rangadih we found an interesting work and to my surprise a man from my home town in Indiana—John Blosser. At this place there is located a church and Bible school. There was not time for a preaching service, but I had the opportunity of visiting the school and of speaking at their chapel. It is strange, yea wonderful, what changes take place in the attitudes and demeanor of people when they become Christians. A person at once feels that he is among friends, and it is evident that "old things are passed away; behold, all things are become new." It was a real pleasure to meet these people, the workers as well as the Indian Christians.

After a good night's rest, and a pleasant half day with the Benedicts and Blossers, we again took up our journey by jeep to Tatanagur where I was to take the train for Champa, the center of the General Conference Mennonite Mission work. Again we drove through a country of low mountains, a bit of paradise in this romantic land. Several of the women from the Rangadih station accompanied us to do some shopping in this large, most westernized city in India where the great Tata steel mills are located. It was evening when we drove up to the station and were hurried on board the train that was on the track waiting for us. I was fortunate in being able to secure an unoccupied compartment and was soon wrapped in my blankets for a night on a springless bed. Early in the morning I was up and out at Champa where Dr. Bauman met me and took me to his home for breakfast.

This mission was started by the late P. A. Penner of Newton, Kansas. For years, in fact during most of its existence, he guided its destiny and directed its development. It stands as a monument to him and his faithful helpers through the years. Their hospital and leper work is outstanding and their evangelistic emphasis is strong. Then began the rounds of a busy day. First on the program was a tour of the institutions. In the afternoon the missionaries from all the stations met for lunch served outside under the trees. During this meeting most of the time was taken up with the discussion of Indianization problems which were so prominent in all mission circles at that time. In the evening we drove to Janjgir some miles away where a strong congregation has been built up and where a Bible School is being maintained. After a good night's rest at the home of these lovely people we were up early for a busy day. At 8:00 A.M. I spoke to the students and faculty of the Bible School, at 9:00 A.M. to the middle school and at 10:00 A.M. to the primary school. In the afternoon at 2:30 there was a church service at which time the

170

large building was filled with people. Then followed a dinner to which some of the prominent men of the community had been invited as guests. After this affair was over we drove out to an evangelistic camp where meetings were in progress. When the singing started the people began to come and after a while a considerable crowd had gathered in the twilight and listened attentively to the messages that were brought from the Word of God. A hasty return brought us back in time for a visit with the judge of the court, a lawyer and an artist, who came in for an evening call. Then followed supper at the women's bungalow where Melva Lehman, Marie Duerksen, and others lived. The next morning at 4:00 A.M. I took the train for Drug where I arrived at noon and was met by the Bauers and later by S. M. King who brought me to Dhamtari for the annual business meeting.

My visit among the stations was at an end. All along the way I found warmhearted Christian men and women who loved the Lord and enjoyed their new experience in the faith. Some of them are descendants of Christian parents whose ancestors have followed the bidding of their Saviour for generations. They are builded on the Rock and have withstood the hardships of the years when it was difficult to uphold their beliefs. Others are newly born children of the kingdom. We found everywhere the problems of a maturing church which confront both the missionaries and the Indians. At times they seem overwhelming and almost beyond solution. But all those who have learned to know God and His marvelous grace have faith to believe that there is a happy answer and that eventually there will emerge a church of Christians that will fit into the Indian environment and serve its purpose. This visit among the churches was the crowning experience of my trip to the Orient and the lovely Indian folk whom I met along the way will always be an inspiration and challenge to my own life. May God keep them until the day of the Great Consummation when together we will meet the Lord in the air and be with Him always!

XVII

THE INSTITUTIONS
OF THE CHURCH IN INDIA

The church of our day needs various kinds of institutions in order to fulfill its entire mission. It needs ways and means whereby it may serve all the needs of mankind—religious, physical, social, intellectual, and economic. This brings with it the opportunity to translate, as it were, the theories of Christian relationships and responsibilities into practical usage. Whatever the attitude of churches sending agencies or missionaries may be when they enter upon the field, they are at once confronted with problems that must be met in a Gospel way. These have to do with health, literacy, means of making a living, and social life.

In an earlier chapter it was stated that the work of the Mennonite Church in India began in a time of famine. This settled the question of the course the missionaries should take, for how could they who had access to this world's goods, shut up their "bowels of compassion" to this great, hungry, suffering, dying multitude? This led to the establishment of orphanages, old people's homes, widows' homes, medical service, and training in the arts of industry the latter of which would enable the people to make a living. A few of these early efforts have now grown into fine institutions—hospitals, leper homes, and schools, including a high school and normal school for the training of teachers. Some of these attempts to help people have declined with the passing of the hunger crisis and a few have been discontinued.

HOSPITALS, DISPENSARIES AND CLINICS

At present the hospital is located at Baithena, a suburb, it may be called, of Dhamtari. Over the years the prejudice against modern medical and surgical service has broken down and the excellent facilities offered at this place are now widely patronized. Each morning long before the time for the hospital to open, patients gather on the compound in front of the dispensary awaiting their turn for treatment. Usually too there are people camping by their oxcarts at the entrance to the grounds, sometimes for hours, waiting for attention.

When we think of institutions of this kind we think of American order and routine with immaculate rooms and wards, and white-clad nurses giving bedside care to inpatients. This picture has to be considerably modified when we speak of the hospital and the service it renders to the Indian public. True, there is what is termed a European ward that bears all the marks of an American ward and carries with it the personal care that we are accustomed to. However, there are very few who have the financial ability to pay the fees for that kind of service. Hence, it is mostly the missionaries and those people of the country who have wealth, that can avail themselves of these facilities. Housing for most of the inpatients is of a different nature altogether. Each one must furnish his own bedding and food. As a rule members of the family or friends do the cooking and otherwise minister to his needs except for the professional care that is required. Surgery and other treatments are administered in accordance with modern medical and sanitary principles and practices. Usually there are several American trained nurses and a larger number of Indian nurses on the staff, all of whom render excellent service.

While in India I witnessed the laying of the foundation for the new hospital. This, I understand, is under construction and part of it may be in use, but the greater part of it still remains unfinished. If the people of America could only see the dire need for these facilities and witness the throngs that daily press to its doors for attention, it is my belief that money would at once become available for the completion of the building and equipment and for the maintenance of the staff.

During the course of its history, nine doctors trained in American medical schools have at various times served in the health program of the mission: Dr. W. B. Page, Dr. C. D. Esch, Dr. Florence Cooprider Friesen, Dr. George D. Troyer, Dr. Fred Brenneman, Dr. J. G. Yoder, Dr. Dana Troyer, Dr. Lillie Kaufman, and Dr. Paul Conrad. In addition to these, Indian trained medical men have served on the medical staff and have rendered valuable service in this field.

In addition to the work at Dhamtari, there is located at Shantipur an excellently equipped institution for the treatment of lepers. This consists of a hospital, hostels, and cottage for the patients. Treatment of those afflicted with this disease began in the early days of the mission. In 1904 the following note was inscribed in the visitors' book by Mr. Thomas Bailey, who was at that time the honorary organizing secretary of the Mission to Lepers in India.

I visited the asylum January 8, 1904, and was greatly impressed with the improvements which have taken place since I was last here. The whole place wore an aspect of brightness and comfort, and the inmates appeared happy and contented which is a great contrast to what one sometimes finds in similar institutions. The homes of the inmates are clean and tidy, and the pretty little garden in front is a great credit to the poor people who work it. Mr. Lapp is to be congratulated on having secured the hearty co-operation of the inmates in carrying on the general management of the institution. From the standpoint of efficiency and economy, this is one of the most satisfying asylums I have yet seen.

This fine compliment to Mahlon Lapp came at a time when housing and other equipment was meager enough. But in spite of those handicaps the government, at this date, began to make per capita contributions for the maintenance of this work. Previously the municipality of Dhamtari had made an appropriation in support of this cause and the Mission to Lepers authorized annual grants of one hundred fifty pounds sterling to care for the immediate wants of these sufferers. From the beginning this institution was in Christian hands and all through its development the right to Christian administration and evangelization was carefully guarded.

In 1924 a new era in this field began. The medical and housing facilities were moved from Dhamtari to Shantipur about four miles away where the modern, well-suited and ample buildings—hospital, dispensary, hostels, and administration—are now located upon spacious and beautiful grounds. The lepers live in cottages and those who are able to do some work may have gardens and fields, goats and chickens. Children attend the schools which are taught by qualified teachers who are afflicted with the disease. Some household industries keep a number of them occupied and contented.

Overshadowing all the other structures is the large, beautiful church where worshipers gather each Lord's day for divine service. What a pathetic and yet inspiring sight it is to see these quiet people gathering into the building and taking their place for worship. I have often heard of their appreciative spirit and their resigned contentment. I have found none in my travels whose faces so beamed with delight at being recognized as did these who were victims of a malady which since ancient times denied them the privilege of mingling freely with mankind. Even Naaman, the mighty field marshal of Syria's host, was not exempt when he was smitten and his fateful plight elicited the sympathy of the captive maid whom he had adopted into his household, and through whose counsel he was healed.

But these two major institutions do not represent all the work that is being done in the field of health and public welfare. Dispensaries are located at a number of stations. At Ghatula, Dondi, Mohadi, Balodgahan, Sankra, and perhaps other places, provisions are made for the treatment of India's diseased and sick and suffering. Roadside clinics for lepers are maintained along the highway between Drug and Sankra. At the time of my visit this work was in charge of S. Paul Miller, one of the missionaries. Early one morning we loaded the car with equipment and medical supplies and started on the wayside tour of mercy. We were accompanied by a compounder who, in our country, would rank somewhat above a trained pharmacist. He is licensed to dispense and within certain limits to administer drugs and medicines. In our company was also an evangelist who regularly went with the workers on their mission of healing. After arrival at the point designated for the meeting of the first group, he gathered the crowd of people together and had a Christian service of song, Scripture reading, prayer and preaching. Meanwhile tables were set up, needles sterilized, and things made ready to begin the day's work. Not only were lepers treated, but also people afflicted with venereal diseases and such other ailments as Mr. Miller and his helper were able to diagnose. From seventy-five to one hundred patients were given care at each of the three stopping places.

This disease is no respecter of rank or social position. At the first station a wealthy family, well-dressed and bedecked with many jewels and other ornaments, sat apart from the others awaiting their turn to be served. At the second place, a wealthy woman or girl, evidently of high standing, richly clad and highly adorned, appeared for treatment. In her exclusiveness she waited patiently for the giant-size needle to puncture her skin and inject into her body the chaulmoogra oil which she hoped would someday make her a well person. Some of these patients have been attending these clinics for years and still remain unhealed. Others have been made well and have again taken their places with the people of the communities where they live. What a wave of gratitude surges through one's soul when he thinks of the conditions that have kept him free from this age-old affliction! What a pity he feels for these poor creatures whose hope still brings them to these gatherings from week to week! Some will no doubt never be healed and will always have to bear the stigma, the limitations, and sufferings which the disease brings with it. But bad and tragic as this malady is, there is something still worse—the leprosy of the soul. If the chaulmoogra oil is of no avail to their mortal bodies, we pray that the "oil of grace" which is being dispensed weekly may bring to them a healing of the spirit. They will then be prepared for the day when the saints will come forth with an incorruptible body, free from every ailment, to join the great white-robed multitude that has been cleansed from every defilement and will then remain where there will be no more discrimination, sadness, or tears.

The dispensaries connected with the mission stations are for the most part in the hands of trained compounders or nurses. In a few places, where such are not available, the missionaries have the work in charge. The united ministry of all these institutions comprises the healing efforts of the church as it serves the needy in the name and spirit of the Master.

EDUCATIONAL INSTITUTIONS

At present there are included in the educational system of the Indian church the following institutions: primary, middle and high schools, the School of Nursing, the Trade School and the Normal School.

At each one of the stations except Dondi, Drug, and Mohadi there are primary schools conducted by the mission and a few are still being maintained in villages apart from the regular stations. Nowhere is the attendance limited to children of Christians. Hindus, Mohammedans and other non-Christians are also admitted and receive the same religious instruction as do those of Christian parents.

As the need for education beyond the primary grades rose, the vernacular middle school was set up in Dhamtari. At this place were located also the hostels for boys and girls who must be absent from their homes during the period of their study. In 1901 the officials of the municipality asked the mission to take over the English school which the city had up to that time maintained. This offer was accepted and the courses were included in the middle school curriculum until 1913 at which time the high school was set up. After many adjustments and additions to the course offerings, the institution was finally in 1931 organized as the Christian Academy and was made to include what was formerly the English Middle School, the High School, the Normal School, and the Bible School. The latter had previously been located at Ghatula.

With this expansion of courses and the consequent increase in enrollment, there rose a need for new buildings. At the time when this situation became urgent, the United States was in the midst of what was perhaps the deepest depression in its history. Money was scarce and hard to get, although the people were gratifyingly responsive to the calls for funds to keep the mission projects going and gave to the work of the church as they could. But the Lord had evidently anticipated this need long before it became apparent to man. Years before a traveler unknown to any of us passed through India visiting missions along the way. He was greatly impressed with the work the Mennonites were doing at Dhamtari and at Champa, the latter of which was operated by the branch of the church to which he belonged. When he returned to his home he wrote his will. Years again passed by. When in the early '20's he died there came to my desk one day a notice from the clerk of the court stating that the India Mission was named in the will as the residuary legatee of this good man's estate.* Owing to some dissatisfaction among the heirs the legacy was withheld, pending a decision of the court, which was not rendered until some time during early '30's. The Board then found itself in possession of some ten thousand dollars. At this same time there came from India an urgent request for a similar amount for the construction of a new high school.

---

* The author was at that time Secretary of the Mennonite Board of Missions and Charities.

With the annual meeting of the Board not far off action was withheld until it was in session, at which time it was voted to set aside the entire amount received from this estate for the erection of this building. How marvelously the Lord leads in devious ways to fulfil the needs of His people!

Since that day the school has grown. In 1930-31 there were thirty-nine students registered of which twelve were Christians, twenty were Hindus, and seven were Mohammedans. In 1950-51 two hundred thirteen were enrolled of which eighty were Christians, one hundred eight Hindus, and five Mohammedans. During my visit at Dhamtari I had the privilege of delivering the address at the dedication of the new Home Economics building. What a satisfaction it was to look over the body of students, faculty, and visitors who were assembled for the occasion and to see the substantial new structure on a beautiful campus! Today this institution is staffed with a faculty of well-trained men and women, nearly all of whom are Christians. All who receive instruction here are taught the Word of God throughout their years of study. Scattered along the road that runs past the compound and over the area surrounding it are the hostels, teachers' houses, and primary schools. Again and again as I passed that way and saw the children going about with their books as they do in other lands and met young people in their classrooms or saw them in their hostels or strolling through the compound, as students always do, I thought of the words "What hath God wrought!"

Another educational unit that is outstanding is the Garjan Memorial School at Balodgahan. It was originally set up to serve the girls of the orphanage. In more recent years it has become co-educational and admits not only resident students but also boys and girls from the surrounding community. It is housed in a beautiful building, situated on a spacious compound surrounded with a brick wall. It is named the Garjan Bai Memorial School in honor of a former member of the faculty who

179

rose from the ranks of a homeless famine waif to become a devoted teacher in the institution, until the time of her death during the flu epidemic in 1918. At the time of my visit Mary M. Good, who has guided its affairs for many years, was in charge. One finds difficulty in visualizing what the condition of all these bright-eyed, keen-minded young people would be had it not been for gifts of life and means which were freely given by Christian friends at home and abroad.

VOCATIONAL SCHOOLS

In the Scripture we read the following words: "Let our people too learn to follow honest occupations for the supply of their necessities, so that they may not lead useless lives" (Titus 3:14, Weymouth translation). From the beginning the missionaries had this principle in mind. In a land like India where many people have difficulty in providing the wherewithal to maintain their existence, the question of how to make a living is an important one. For this reason vocational training was early introduced as a part of the program of the church. In an article "Our Mission Schools and the Community," S. M. and Nellie King have the following to say:

The emphasis on practical training has been felt throughout the years and at various times industrial schools have been provided for both boys and girls. But some of these attempts were short-lived for such reasons as lack of personnel, lack of equipment, and even for lack of interest on the part of those for whom the school was opened.

The most successful attempt along this line was in the training of carpenters. This project was kept going in co-operation with the government until 1946. During the period of its existence it turned out men who are now in business for themselves and are successful. As one sees the beautiful furniture such as chairs, tables, wardrobes, dressers, and sideboards, which were made by the boys in the school or by those who received their training there, he wishes it were possible to have things so beautiful in his own home.

THE SCHOOL OF NURSING

The latest venture in the field of education is the establishment of a school for the training of nurses. This is in its infancy and depends for its success upon several things. First, adequate facilities in connection with the hospital which will enable the students to secure the practical training and clinical experience that is needed to prepare them for their profession; second, an adequate teaching staff consisting of qualified nurses; and third, living quarters for the students. In India, as elsewhere, such institutions cannot be self-sustaining and this new venture will have to depend on aid from the home church in order to provide all the facilities necessary for its successful operation. But what a blessing it will be to the girls who desire to enter this field which is one of the noblest of all professions open to women! Its benefit to the hospital, its patients, the medical staff, and the community, cannot be measured. And last, but surely not least, those who will go into homes of their own will have the knowledge that will enable them to do for their families the things that are so much needed in a land where sanitation, dietary problems, and other health helps have for so long been neglected.

INSTITUTIONS OF CHARITY

From the beginning the church in India has concerned itself with the needs of homeless and indigent people. It has always cared for orphans and sometimes had as many as six hundred of these unfortunate waifs on its hands. Earlier the girls' orphanage was located at Rudri, but when those buildings were taken over by the government, the institution was moved to Balodgahan where at the time of my visit there were some eighty girls in the home. The one for boys is located in Dhamtari and serves also as a home for boarding students from the villages or homes

181

outside of Dhamtari. The home for blind and crippled old men was established in 1919. At that time there were twenty-seven inmates. This number has now decreased to two or three. The Widows Industrial Home has been a haven of refuge for helpless and unfortunate women who became victims of the social customs of their land and had nothing to look forward to but hardship and difficulty. It is now located at Balodgahan and shelters some fifty people. Some of them are old and are unable to do much. Others are younger and are able to work. They like to help in the fields and about the compound. One of them has charge of the flock of geese which belongs to the mission. At harvesttime they work in the rice and during the season they help with the gardening. Some have learned to make rugs and do needlework, others help care for the babies that are brought to the Babies' Home.

All of these institutions, whether educational, industrial, or charitable rose out of some need which gave the missionaries the opportunity of ministering to helpless and impoverished people in the spirit of the Master. No doubt these extra tasks have added to the burdens and cares of the workers but when one sees what has been accomplished, he cannot but feel that it has all been worth while.

After this hasty review one begins to wonder about the future of the mission and missionaries in that land. Ever since I have been in a position where I heard about the hopes of the missionaries, they have spoken longingly of the day when the Indian church can take over its work and go on. This time has now arrived. The spirit of independence that swept over the country during the last few decades and came to its climax at the close of the war has reached into the church. The membership feels that it should have a voice in the management of all ecclesiastical and institutional affairs. Others wonder whether the people are ready to take over such responsibility. However this problem may be worked out, the result must eventually be that the church will be one brotherhood consisting of missionaries, Indian people, and those of other nationalities all of whom have an equal voice in the management of its affairs. The lines which now exist will eventually have to be obliterated. This will, no doubt, involve changes. Whatever new buildings are erected will likely be such as the Indians can construct and maintain. It will mean less imposing structures, and we with our western sense of what is orderly will probably have to be satisfied with less than our ideals call for. In the end it will be a national church upholding the teachings of the Scripture and its practices in such a way that it will serve their people and in a manner in which they can serve the cause for which they stand. And we, as helpers, will share with them our resources as we do with our own here in America and help them to build a glorious church which will be acceptable to Him who "hath made of one blood all nations of men for to dwell on all the face of the earth" and has redeemed us all by His grace.

XVIII

INDIA
WHAT OF THE NIGHT

Can the New India survive the storms and stress of the time into which it was born? This question is upon many lips today. Its birth took place when governments were tottering under burdens such as people who are now living have not witnessed before. That is still true. Financial loads of unmeasured greatness stare in the face nations that but a few years ago were considered sound. Those who were once the bankers of the world are now on the border of insolvency. Others have launched out on "daring" and untrodden paths that raise alarming concerns about the outcome of their ventures. Established diplomatic procedures which were built up over the centuries and had been long accepted, seem to have been discarded, and instead procedures with no regard for order have raised their ugly heads. In many places national honor and personal integrity are at the lowest ebb and many folks in responsible places are not too much concerned about it. Nationalism, selfishness, and greed seem to be enthroned and are riding furiously to accomplish their ends. Can a country that is just "learning to walk" survive with all the problems it has inherited from the past, as well as those that are thrust upon it by the conditions under which it lives? The world looks on with hopeful eyes and welcomes this newcomer into world affairs, praying that it may have the needed wisdom, understanding, and patience in order to make its position secure in the family of nations.

India is a land hoary with age. Its people were cultured and civilized while our forebears in Gaul worshiped at the shrines of Thor and perhaps dined on the flesh of their enemies. It has its past to deal with. In its traditions are wrapped up its religions with its caste which separates people from each other and sets up barriers that are difficult to remove even though they are by legislation declared abolished. It has its age-old mores and folkways that reach to the most remote villages of the plain and jungle, where reinforced by superstition and prejudice they become almost insurmountable blocks that obstruct the way of change to better things.

Then too, it for some reason missed the ennobling influence of early Christianity which began in Palestine at the time when the knowledge of God as it was known to Abraham attained its fullest and highest manifestation in the divine Son when the "Word became flesh, and dwelt among us." Perhaps this was because military and political power had gravitated westward and at the time of the Saviour's birth it resided in the Empire that had its seat at Rome from which might and order flowed. With this shift of the center of authority and domination came intellectual enlightenment, stability of government, and safety of travel on land and sea, all of which made it possible for Christianity with its elevating influence and power to spread and thrive until its place in the Occident became secure. The Orient deprived of this potent force, which the West so often misappropriated, misused and misapplied, followed its own lines of development in government and in the economic, moral, and social order. There are claims of the Apostle Thomas having visited India and establishing a church which still exists, but the great stream of Christian influence in that early day followed the open lanes of travel westward where its teaching, experience, and the environment in which it developed determined what the Christian church should be.

But India has other problems which were thrust upon her from the outside. Centuries ago western nations began to cast envious eyes upon the far eastern countries, invaded them for selfish ends, brought them into subjection, and far too often exploited them and imposed upon them not the best they had to offer but the worst. Africa became spoken of as the "Dark Continent" not alone because of the ignorance and depravity of its native population but also because of what Europe and America contributed to its awfulness through their slave traders and through their gold-hungry marauders, adventurers, and soldiers of fortune. The same may be said of India as well as of the newly discovered lands of the west, the Latin Americas. No doubt the native religions of many of these newly acquired possessions made room for degrading moral practices and ways of life, and concerned themselves little with poverty, disease, or economic problems. So did the conquistadors who were concerned only with their own interests and took little or no account of the needs of the indigenous population. India became spoken of as a "Benighted Land" in a manner that made one feel that all its troubles had been fostered by its own, little realizing or admitting that the ravenous outlanders who entered the country had all too often contributed greatly toward its burden.

The one ray of light, the trickling of an elevating influence from the outside, came with the missionaries. They preached the unsearchable riches of God in Christ Jesus, redemption from sin, and a way of life that leads to higher and better things. They also taught that all men are equal, that God "hath made of one blood all nations of men for to dwell on all the face of the earth, and hath determined the times before appointed and the bounds of their habitation." This was no doubt often better preached than practiced. The new doctrine did, however, concern itself with the welfare of the whole person—body, mind, and soul. With it came institutions and a type of ministry hitherto little known among these people: schools, hospitals, homes for the indigent, trade schools, and churches.

England's struggle for supremacy in India was a long, arduous, and continuous one. Its first contest was with the Dutch and French to decide who was to be master in this land of fabled wealth that was known even before the days of Solomon's greatness. Having settled this question, it proceeded to establish itself through the East India Trading Company, to whom powers of control were intrusted. At the outset, it is said, this organization "enjoyed power and profit without responsibility." Its major purpose for coming into the country was profit. After years of troublous rule it was finally and definitely subordinated to the British Crown and made in essence a department of state. The reasons for this were evident. The Company's government of the natives had greatly reduced the lucrative dividends of its shareholders. Besides it had been arrogating power after power unto itself until it became virtually an Empire within an Empire, and England as a nation was, in the eyes of the onlookers, being charged as a sharer in its agent's sins. Lastly there was a rising moral reaction in India and in Britain against the excesses which continued throughout the land.

Protests, dissatisfaction, and prejudice against foreign rule led to the mutiny of 1857 which was precipitated by disciplinary action taken by the British against several companies of cavalry because they refused to comply with an order that involved the violation of one of their religious principles. This resulted in fighting of unmeasured savagery on both sides. An entire garrison of soldiers and their families were massacred at Cawnpore. The British retaliated with measures of equal ferocity. By the end of the year, so authorities say, the rebellion was suppressed and the mutinous forces were brought under control, except for the bitter feeling that continued.

It is not easy, says a native author, for an Indian to write about the rebellion of 1857, of its blood and tears and its suffering, heroism and humiliations. Until India regains her freedom, the writing will never be free from emotional overtones. "1857" strikes a flint of his heart and sparks fly. With an obstinate silence we have refected and passed by the spate of literature on the

Mutiny that has come from British writers. It, however, continues to stalk through our memory—an unavenged and unappeased ghost!

In confirmation of this testimony of an Indian who speaks for his people, several Englishmen quote the following lines from the writings of Hardy.

> Nought remains,
> But the vindictiveness here among the strong
> and there amid the weak an impotent rage.

This incident climaxed the end of the East India Company's authority. In 1858 an act for the better government of the country was passed by the British Parliament by which all authority and power was transferred to the Crown. A Viceroy was then appointed to be the head of the new government by which this part of Britain's domain was to be ruled. In the performance of his duties the governor was assisted by a Council of five, all of whom were originally British. It was not until 1909 that the natives were given representation in this body. In 1877 Queen Victoria was proclaimed Empress of India and this land of romance and beauty became a part of the Empire upon which the sun never sets.

This change in governmental affairs, however, did not solve all of the country's problems. To an onlooker, who is not steeped in the lore of British-Indian affairs, it appears that on the whole the English tried to govern well and to administer justice equitably and considerately. They labored long and diligently on a Penal Code that took account of India's peculiar conditions and needs. They have the satisfaction of having competent authorities say that this represented an almost ideal system of laws and legal procedures. Judges and jurists of highest integrity were appointed to preside over the courts and bring to all the diverse races and people the advantage of the great principle of equality before the bar, regardless of their social and racial status or the divisions created by the caste system.

During this final period of rule the British no doubt tried to undo the mistakes of the earlier regime and build up good will among the people. But the past was too heavily loaded with grievances, injustice, and bitter memories to be so lightly satiated or to be so soon forgotten. Beside these there were other factors that always loomed large in the situation. There was the inevitable clash of culture and religion. The English never identified themselves socially with the native population but maintained an aloofness which men of no less renown than Nehru declared to be the introduction of a new caste into the social strata of the country. Large masses of the people remained untouched by the benevolent movements and improvements which the new order introduced. Within the masses there was a growing group of intellectuals who were trained in the best institutions of Europe and America. Professional and businessmen also were conscious of themselves and of their powers. As one reads the history of this period he is made to feel their deep longing for self rule, even though many who talked about it little knew what would be involved should their desires be granted. Ideas of self government became stronger with the years and refused to remain suppressed or squelched by any force or movement from the outside or by any which was fostered by native princes and landholders, kings and kinglets on the inside.

But greater than the influence of political and intellectual enlightenment of its time, some commentators think, was the spiritual revival that rose in Hinduism during the latter part of the nineteenth century. In spite of the work of Christian missionaries, many of the natives considered the western culture a soul-less and materialistic philosophy. The past and its culture was idealized. The following lines taken from an Indian newspaper of that period indicate something of the spirit that prevailed.

The motherland is the symbol of our National idea . . . the Divine idea, the Logos, which has been revealing itself through the entire course of our past historic evaluation. The motherland is really the syntheses of all the Goddesses that have ever been and are still being worshipped by Hindus.

Of this class Swami Dayanand Saraswati became the champion and leader. He is generally considered as the founder of the movement of the new Nationalism based on the teachings of the ancient Vedas, where he found no practice of caste or polytheism or idolatry or child-marriages. He was born into a well-to-do family and might well have enjoyed all the benefits of an English education and all the privileges that were open to those of his class, but he renounced them all—family, wealth, and position—and chose rather the life of a homeless ascetic. To him everything foreign was evil. He considered modern Hinduism corrupt and sought to free it from its caste and evil practices by preaching a primitive and purified form of the ancient faith of his fathers.

Swami Vivekananda gave impetus to the movement of Indian nationalism. He spoke before the Parliament of Religions at the Chicago World's Fair in 1893. He claimed to speak for the Mother of Religions and turned for his text to the following extract from one of the Vedic hymns.

As the different streams, having their sources in different places, all mingle their waters in the sea, so, O Lord, the different paths which men take through different tendencies, various though they appear, crooked or straight, all lead to Thee.

This address was received with a great ovation at the assembly where it was delivered and made a deep impression upon the audience. That the great mass of Hindus do not agree with a view so liberal, is well confirmed by the extremely antagonistic attitude they take toward anyone who endeavors to lead them away from their faith and bring them into the fellowship of Christians or any other religious group. Encouraged by the reception of his message in the United States this Indian orator returned to his homeland and began preaching the doctrine of a militant Nationalism, reinforced with his own religious concepts.

Once more the world must be conquered by India. This is the great ideal before us. Let them come and flood the land with their armies, never mind! Up India and conquer the world with your spirituality! Spirituality must conquer the west. Where are the men ready to go out to every country in the world with the message of the great sages of India? There is no other alternative —we must do it or die. The only condition of national life, once more vigorous national life, is the conquest of the world by Indian thought.

It is conceded by authorities that messages such as this did a great deal to strengthen the position of the ancient religions and did not enhance the popularity of the strangers who had imposed themselves upon the country. The glory of their past was revived and a new self-respect arose. It aroused a belief in the future and resulted in a wave of enthusiasm that some commentators claim to have been the beginning of the remaking of India.

A movement so virile and active as this and so much in contradiction with what the second largest religious group in India, the Mohammedans, believed and practiced, could not go unnoticed. But while the Hindus were carried along on the wave of the Renaissance the Moslems passed under a cloud. They were made to bear the brunt of the blame for the Great Mutiny of 1857. They refrained from taking advantage of the educational opportunities of the time and consequently were not qualified to take the positions which were open in the government, or to enter the professions as the young Hindus were. Their attitude toward taking usury barred them from some lines of business. A writer of the early 30's of the last century sums up the situation as follows:

While Bengali Hindu, Madrisis, and Marathas inspired by the arts and sciences of Europe were experiencing an intellectual and moral renaissance, the Muslims all over India were falling into a state of material indigence and intellectual decay.

It was some thirty years later that this group found a voice in the person of Sir Seyed Ahmad Khan. After a visit to England he returned to his people with a message designed to stir them out of their lethargy.

I am not thinking about things in which, owing to the specialties of our respective countries, we and the English differ. I only remark on politeness, knowledge, good faith, cleanliness, skilled workmanship, accomplishment and thoroughness, which are the results of education and civilization. All good things, spiritual and worldly, which should be found in man, have been bestowed by the Almighty on Europe, and especially on England.

Shades of Mohamet! What would he say to this? What do Sir Seyed's coreligionists think today?

He urged a regeneration of the religious life of his people and insisted on education as the means by which it might be accomplished. Through his influence the pro-British Aligarh Anglo-Oriental College, patterned after Oxford and Cambridge, was founded. He was keenly conscious of the minority position of his group, and because of this limitation he placed himself on record as being opposed to a popular electoral system. In 1906 the All-India Muslim League was founded in order to unify the Mohammedans and set them up as a block against Hindu influence and power which was becoming increasingly active in the Nationalistic Movement of that time.

Toward the close of the nineteenth century things began to happen that cast a cloud upon the hitherto unchallenged supremacy of Europe. In the last decade of the century the Italian forces suffered complete defeat at the hands of Abyssinian warriors. The stout resistance of the Boers to British armies in South Africa showed that the weak colonials were forces that had to be reckoned with. But the sleep of the centuries was broken when news spread over the world that the Japanese, a small Asiatic people, had resoundingly defeated the hosts of the great Russian Empire which even the British at that time considered the arch-enemy of their own. Then came the first World War with its barbarous machines of destruction, its devastation and loss of life, and finally Versailles where western statesmanship showed its mediocrity by bringing forth a treaty designed to assure peace but which produced instead a crop of "Dragon's teeth." One cannot but believe that out of it came conditions that made possible the last and most terrible of all wars. The vice-president of one of America's largest universities who visited the Far East in the early thirties, made the following statement upon his return:

The East lost its fear of the West as a result of the Russian-Japanese War. The West lost its influence in the East during the World War and its respect as a result of the movies.

What an indictment!

The record of Britain's rule in India throughout all its history indicates a rather uneasy control. At times the surface appeared calm, but even so evidences of discontent were ever present beneath the surface. There were periodic outbreaks of violence, terror, bloodshed, mutinies, strikes, protests, petitions, civil disobedience, and passive resistance. The English will not soon forget the Black Hole of Calcutta, the Mutiny of 1857, and other acts of savagery perpetrated by the Indians. Nor will the latter forget the retaliating measures inflicted by the British, who countered with armies, deportations, imprisonment, legislation, conferences, and promises of improvement intended to satisfy and control the turbulent element in the population.

But still India was not satisfied! It wanted its independence. Experience had convinced it, no doubt, that victory by the use of armies would not be possible. At that juncture there emerged a little man—the Mahatma Gandhi who became the great leader of the masses. Instead of depending upon the physical might of the people he proceeded to muster its spiritual resources and when freedom came it was not on the field of battle but at the council table overshadowed by this fasting ascetic whose spirit controlled the soul of India.

When the British sailed away they did not take with them all of the country's problems. While the new government was struggling with the affairs of the infant nation, rumblings of discontent were beginning to be heard. Gandhi and his followers had hoped for a united people. But the Mohammedans, still conscious of their minority, came forth with plans to strengthen their position. Some spoke of a divided nation—one Hindu, the other Muslim. It was at this point that the voice of an immaculately dressed, Oxford trained, Bombay lawyer, Mahomed Ali Jinnah, leader of the All-India Muslim League who stood high in the councils of his people, spoke and rallied the forces of independence for the events of Direct Action Day which was set for August, 1946. "We will have either a divided India or a destroyed India" was his terrifying conclusion.

The appalling events that led to the setting up of the new state in the northern provinces had their beginning at Calcutta, but before the struggle was over it reached across the country from the east to the west. Such a holocaust of suffering, bloodshed, death, hunger, disease, and despair as followed in the wake of vast migrations of uprooted and displaced people—Hindus, Mohammedans, Sikhs, and others—who drifted across the land does not belong to an age such as ours. One wonders whether perhaps these "Children of the Sun" in the Far East took their cue from us who have set them a gruesome example of how wrongs should be righted and of how differences should be adjudicated. We then stand mutely by for when we protest spectres rise from the ash piles of our creation and to our ears come the reverberating echoes of the cries of despair from ruins we have made!

Today the British are gone, the nation is divided. Each one, India and Pakistan, is trying to find its way in a world that is torn by strife and conflicting ideologies, as it has not been for centuries. Suspicion and distrust reign everywhere. Arrogance is deeply rooted and holds sway in many places. Governments that were formerly considered as stable as Gibraltar are tottering. Some have fallen and others have given place to new and violent forms of rule and of social control. Finances are unstable—just where is the nation that is sure of its fiscal soundness? In wide areas age-old economic orders have been dissolved or are in the process. Enemies with "dripping jaws" are prowling under cover—some in the open—seeking the life of these newly born children among the nations and one may well ask, "India; What of the Night?" As one among the older brothers we extend them a helping hand to guide them through the dangers of their new venture and wish them Godspeed on their way to become great in the things that make for greatness—righteousness, justice, equality, and above all, the goodness that only God can bestow!

But India has other problems besides those that pertain to the affairs of state and its relation to other nations. It has its masses that run into hundreds of millions that have to be fed. In the Orient the matter of food is a problem of proportions which we of the Western Hemisphere have never known. In this new nation as in every other land this is tied up with the soil. It is said that the peasants of the densely populated Far Eastern countries never have more than one year's supply between themselves and famine, and sometimes not more than a day. It is no wonder, then, that the humble ryot looks back into the golden age of the past, as he thumbs his Vedas that sing of the time when hunger was no more known among the poor than it was among the rich:

We had corn in our granaries, our tanks were filled with fish, and the eye was soothed and refreshed with the limpid blue of the sky and the green foliage of the trees. All day long the peasant toiled in the field, and at eve, returning to his lamplit home, he sang the song of his heart.

India has much good land, but most of it is in the possession of the few. This trend constitutes an old, old problem. Moses was warned of it at the borders of Palestine when the hosts of Israel were about to cross the Jordan into their promised possession. Provision was wisely made for the control of the economy of his time by setting up laws which were designed to make it impossible for people to become permanently alienated from their land. Every fiftieth year it was to be returned to the family to which it was originally allotted. But in spite of such an arrangement the prophets speak of the rich having added "house to house," and "field to field" until there was no room for the poor upon the soil from which they draw their livelihood.

If the ancient writers of the Vedas represent conditions correctly then something like Israel's experiences must have happened in India between Vedic times and the present. Most of the land is now in the hands of large holders and as in Bible times there is no room for the great bulk of the people except as serfs or servants. How to settle this problem has baffled the minds of administrators in all countries for many years. Communal societies such as the Zoarites, the Owenites, the Amanites, the Hutterites and others have tried the plan of having all things in common. All of these schemes with the exception of the Hutterites have been abandoned. Russia has set up what is called a Communistic order but which is in reality none other than a capitalistic state which owns the land and defines the conditions under which its people may derive the use or benefit of it.

The new India is facing this same problem now. What can be done for the great mass of hungry and landless which fill the country? Shall the state take over the land and distribute it to the poor? If it does, on what basis shall the owner be compensated and who will pay the price? No doubt if and when such measures shall be put into action those questions along with many others will loom large in a nation whose treasury is taxed to the limit with other affairs.

Perhaps some messenger will again come forth from the

desert and Gandhi-like lay the problem upon the hearts of the people who have the possessions and inspire them to share their holdings with those who have nothing. Maybe the little ninety-pound ascetic, Acharya Vinoba Bhave, with sandaled feet, clad only in waist cloth, the "god," they call him, "who gives away land," has the answer. He walks from village to village and appeals to the goodness in human nature to share their holding with those whose hands are empty. Will he succeed in his mission? It is said that in response to his appeals the landlords have given their tenants more than thirty-five thousand acres without coercion or without payment. This frail little man, unkempt, half-naked, jailed a half dozen times for conducting a passive-resistance campaign against England when it entered World War II, may have the solution to one of the nation's major problems. He may also have the antidote to Communism, which usually looks better to people before they are drawn into it than afterwards.

Can the new state handle these and the multitude of other difficulties with which it is confronted in its attempt to set itself upon its feet? In the midst of uncertainty can she attract capital from the outside or that which is stored inside her domain, to develop resources, many of which still await the mind of a master to bring forth their treasures and prepare them for the use of mankind. Can she maintain peaceful relations without and within at this time, against the forces that seek to engulf her? She has already accomplished what other nations have not been able to. America paid for her freedom from British domination with the blood of her sons. India, after a long struggle and various experiments, finally accomplished the same ends through passive means. Russia and her satellites have broken up the large real estate holdings by violence and forceful measures of confiscation. India is approaching this problem with some success by an appeal to the human sense of justice, asking men to share their holdings with the poor. Perhaps this new-born

197

nation can show the world the way out of its dilemma. We bid her Godspeed and pray for her success. While she is raising her ensign high and marshaling all her powers for the struggle, we hear the watchman cry: India! What of the night? The world is waiting for the answer!

XIX

GLIMPSES
ALONG INDIA'S HIGHWAYS

These are gleanings from among the observations and experiences of a traveler along the highroads of India. They have no relation to the problems that now confront the country politically, socially, or religiously. Rather, they are episodes which constitute the spice with which arduous tasks are flavored as one travels to and fro in strange places, among strange people, who live in surroundings that are new to the foreigner. To those who have always lived in those parts of the world distant from us, such things are a part of the common, everyday, humdrum affairs of life, but to the alien they are new. During my tenure as Secretary of the Mission Board I always looked forward with interest to the first letters from new missionaries. They teemed with observations, incidents, and experiences that were strange and fresh in their minds. Within a few years they became too ordinary to receive passing notice. By the time they had spent their term of six and one-half years in the country the things that were at first so interesting and charming, or perhaps even frightening, had lost their luster and were relegated to the commonplace. After that those that were of greater value, came to the front and brought other interests to the fore which occupied the time and thought of those whom the years of service had matured.

India cannot be separated from the unusual. Its snake and tiger stories, elephants, monkeys and the multitude of other things that are part of the life of the country, are new and ever intriguing to us who live in the luridness of our hurried western world. The snake stories range all the way from escapades with the fiery, aggressive cobra, which is always ready for a combat, to the docile but venomous krite that in some manner manages to slither up walls, door jams, or crevices and has the uncomfortable habit of falling off the lintel on a person's neck. The giant python when full grown can swallow a small goat on one long, laborious gulp, and somehow manage to live, even though the indigestible ribs of its victim may puncture holes into its slimy sides as it makes its way through its digestive canal.

My first encounter with a snake charmer came in Karachi. He was seated on the sidewalk in a corner of a building with his deadly cobra in a neatly covered basket and was soliciting coins for a performance. Once an adequate number had been tossed into his lap, he uncovered the container and the head of the performing reptile popped up. This subtle, lethal creature which certainly has no love for the human race, uncoiled itself with its spreading head erect and surveyed its surroundings. When the first note of the flute was sounded its hood flattened as though it was about to strike but as the sounds deepened its body swayed with the rhythm of the music. When its master concluded that his audience had received its money's worth, he, with one swift movement of his hand, caught the enchanted creature by that part of its anatomy which would pass for the neck in any other animal and put it back into its basket. What a gruesome business this snake charming is! Some people say they are beautiful but that all sinks into emptiness when considered in the lights of its record from Eden on. Since that fatal episode in the Garden, its venom-filled head has been a symbol of all that is evil—Satan, sin, guile, deception, and death. Let them that will risk their lives to gather in such a repulsive fashion the coins they need to live by. The rest of us will bestow our energy and our pice and annas and rupees upon a better cause.

In America the monkeys are in the zoo. In India they run

wild and go by families and colonies. Because they are held sacred by the Hindus they enjoy the protection of the law. Whenever the group becomes too large, the government sends out its officials to round them up and ship a portion of the horde to another place where they are again turned loose on the helpless public. Here they will carry on as before, scampering across the house roofs or thronging the rice fields or climbing trees for fruit. They become very destructive in gardens and in general make a nuisance of themselves in spite of their humorous antics.

I had never seen a colony of them unrestrained and in their native habitat and was beginning to wonder whether I might finish my travels across the country without catching even a glimpse of them. Then one morning while driving along a jungle road we saw a group of a half dozen or so hovering around the edge of a forest but they were too far away to afford us a good look. But the longed-for opportunity came one evening when we were returning from the leper clinic. A family of them had taken possession of a strip of riceland and the long-tailed youngsters were having a field day. The old mother sat high up in a tree where she could enjoy the hilarity of her carousing brood. Some were hanging by their tails on the branches—perhaps they were being punished for misbehavior. Others were chasing their brothers and sisters through the treetops and hopping across the rice fields wreaking havoc with the crop that was about to be harvested. Occasionally one stopped, in what appeared to be a game, to heave clods of earth or stones at his fleeing companions.

When our station wagon was brought to a halt the grizzled old sire of the "clan" made his way slowly and deliberately along the rice bank to within a few rods—perhaps within eight or ten—from where we were and sat down to evaluate the situation. Perhaps he remembered the story of the kidnaping of Sita, the beautiful wife of the Prince of Ayodhya, long ago by peculiar strangers who carried her off in some strange vehicle and he was going to make sure that these pale people traveling in such an unusual contraption would not make off with his spouse or any of the numerous members of his family. I "unlimbered" my photographic apparatus and made my way cautiously toward him, hoping that he would not become scared and retreat beyond the range of the camera. His face was far from handsome to begin with and his appearance did not improve as I approached him. He bared his teeth and gave me the most unwelcome, ungracious, arrogant, challenging, defiant, and ugly look I ever received from anyone. I had nothing but the best of intentions and what I had done to so upset this old patriarch of monkeydom and stir up such a spirit of animosity is something I perhaps will never be able to ascertain. I presume I don't understand monkeys. I know something of the disposition of those bipeds throughout the world that act like monkeys but the rude conduct of this Indian savage is beyond my comprehension. Whatever his motive may have been, he missed having his picture taken.

But snakes and monkeys are not the only denizens of the jungle and grasslands of India that challenge the curiosity of the newcomer and call for his admiration or contempt. In the woods the peacocks spread their tail feathers widely and adorn the place with their glory. Deer—beautiful, agile, and curious, lurk within the shadows and hide their mottled coats in the lights and shades of the trees and shrubs. Wild boars, that look like a close relative of the Missouri razor-backs roam through the land and live on the nuts, twigs, and whatever else they find for food. But of most interest as well as dread are the large felines, the tigers, the leopards, and other cats, that haunt these wilds and stir one's desire to catch a glimpse of them as they are in their native home. In spite of all the damage they do and of all the tales of their ferocity one hears, people who live as neighbors with them say that they are not as fierce and dangerous as one might conclude from the stories that circulate about them. Those who are in a position to know say they will not likely molest human beings unless they are attacked or cornered or wounded, except when no other food is available or when on account of their age they find it difficult to catch other game. I was always very skeptical of such stories and am yet, but the edge of my doubts was somewhat dulled since that evening when we, Wilbur Hostetler and his family and I, drove his jeep along a jungle road. Some little distance ahead of us—perhaps forty or fifty rods—we saw one of these large beasts crossing the road. He was beautifully striped and made his way catlike into the bushes on the other side. When we came to the place where he had entered the forest we stopped and found that his curiosity, like ours, had gotten the best of him, and had made him bold to halt and observe what was going on. He was not more than twenty or thirty feet away from us. No one could have asked for a better pose than he had taken. We looked at each other until he was satisfied, then with his head down and his nose nearly to the ground he trotted off leisurely into the woods.

How beautiful this wild life is in its native habitat! I have seen specimens of all kinds in the zoo but they are a suppressed and pitiful lot. The fire has gone out of their nature and the graceful swing of their movements has disappeared. I have seen the thousands of wild horses that covered the range of our western grazing lands and saw them, glorious in their appearance, go pell-mell with the freedom of the wind at the approach of horsemen. But when confined to the corral or subdued to the harness their spirit is crushed, the light goes out of their eyes, and they lumber along with all the enthusiasm of their lightsome life burned out. The coyote that charms the plainsmen of our land with his long weird notes at eventime or the jackals of India's plains, the "evening wolves" of the Old Testament, swing across space with an ease and grace that makes one feel like a sinner to reduce them to slavery where the luster of their eyes is dimmed to a glassy stare and their movements seem without aim or purpose and become almost painful.

203

A person would hardly dare return from India without having participated in a tiger hunt. My first experience took place soon after my arrival. One day Arnold Deitzel and Ralph Smucker, an accomplished marksman, and I visited Mangal Tarai, the center of the symptom-free leper colony. After our visit was finished it was suggested that we go hunting. The jungle adjoining the colony is at the edge of tiger-infested territory. Some months before Dr. Yoder had shot a large male in this area. For many nights after that the villagers heard the doleful call of his mate who vainly sought for her companion. Almost every day evidences of the presence of these marauders appear and when darkness falls, the natives say, one can hear their playful noises or hunger cries in the near-by woods. The prospect of a successful drive seemed hopeful. But the venture was a disappointment. We saw the woodland roads and trails leading to villages and even met some people, but no wild life of any kind.

But a real hunt was scheduled at the same place the day before I left Dhamtari to begin my journey back to the States. Early one morning, equipped with food, rifles, and ammunition we left for the hunting scene. Somewhere around one hundred or more men were on hand to serve as "beaters." It was their business to scare out the game and drive it toward the stations where marksmen with rifles were located. Everybody was eager to start. We covered one section of the timber in the forenoon which yielded one peahen about the size of a turkey. That, in fact, happened before the hunt began. After lunch the drive was taken up in another section of the jungle. A number of times deer passed our station but it seemed that there were no cats or if there were any they were securely hidden where noises did not disturb them. Finally the prospect became so unpromising that R. R. Smucker, whom I was with, did not think it worth while to even take the ordinary precautions of climbing a tree for safety. While he was on the ground loitering almost indifferently behind some bushes, a beautiful leopard came out of the woods, crossed the road, and took a course leading in our direction. This I thought was our chance to get a good skin to take home. The excitement and the prospect of success set my nerves tingling. All my hope was staked on Smucker's marksmanship but the shot from his German Mauser was too high. With one wide leap the animal changed his course and was lost in the woods. Later this same cat was seen again in another sector of the forest but the chance of laying him low was gone.

But not all the incidents that fall under one's observation along the highways have to do with snakes, snake charmers, tigers and leopards, peacocks and wild life. There are other interests of higher value and greater inspiration. Some years ago when a noted layman, who was connected with a widely known business concern, returned from India he was asked what was the most wonderful thing he saw. He presumed, so he said, that people would expect him to talk about snakes and tigers, the splendor of the Taj Mahal or the massive Himalayas or any one of the many other wonders of this enchanted land. Instead, he related the following incident. One morning, he said, when he and his driver entered a village of South India, they saw an old man with leprous sores on his body. His eyesight was gone and his face disfigured with scars of the disease. Some toes and fingers were missing too. He was sitting on the ground outside of his hut absorbing the warmth of the morning sun. When this traveler stopped and inquired about his welfare, his poor, disfigured face lit up with a smile benign and he began to enumerate the many things he had to be thankful for. He spoke of friends who gave him a home and food. He related the joys of being a Christian, the hope of a home beyond, and the many, many spiritual blessings that made his life bearable since he found a Saviour. He was one of a great brotherhood that reached around the world. This, said that businessman, was the most wonderful thing he saw in all his travels. No doubt there are many more who would be able to bear such testimony. A healing of the soul that makes it possible to look into darkness each day with a body filled with sores that know no healing and a life of emptiness save for the hope of what the future in Christ Jesus holds for men is the highest of all attainments possible. Are not such things as these what our Saviour had in mind when He said to His disciples after His experience with the lame man at the pool, "And he will shew him greater works than these, that ye may marvel." Joy and satisfaction such as this come to those as have found peace and contentment in spite of diseased and pain-racked bodies.

One evening while at my room on Mission Road in Calcutta an outburst of song led me hurriedly to the window to see what was going on. Below on the sidewalk a small group was singing Gospel hymns. Beautiful voices filled the air and made their surroundings ring with melodies of the songs of Zion. People were gathering until the street was practically blocked. Among them were those who bore the marks of the saints of God. According to the testimony which some of them gave they had been redeemed from sin and were happy members of the white-robed throng that await His coming in glory. Others listened intently. Some mocked as they always do and walked away. But the Word was preached which long ago the prophet said "shall not return unto . . . [Him] void." This is but one of the places where such incidents occur. Day by day souls are being gathered, one by one, from here and there and added to the kingdom of heaven. This has been going on every day since the Gospel was first proclaimed by the Master Himself, and shall, we hope, continue till He comes again.

In South India there is a body of Christians that claim to be the survivors of the ministry of the Apostle Thomas, one of Christ's chosen twelve who went into that part of the world with the tidings of salvation. In more recent years, the last century and a half, as a result of hard work, often violent opposition, loneliness, discouragement, and defeat some six million more have been added to the ranks of what is now a stable, growing body of Christians that is becoming conscious of its responsibility, its strength, and its life. May we not neglect to extend to them the hand of fellowship and Christian brotherliness and help them as they gird themselves for the tasks that lie ahead in a world where the gloom and shadows of sin seem to be deepening. They are our spiritual kinsmen, our brothers in Christ, redeemed by the same Saviour, cleansed by the same blood, and sanctified by the same Spirit. While the day lingers on in which we can work may we not neglect to go with them to the task and labor side by side until the day closes and the brightness of His coming appears.

This chapter, however, cannot be brought to a close without a word about the fellowship with the missionaries, all of whom are struggling not only with the problems of sin and the task of evangelization but also with the problems of a maturing church, a changing political economy and questions of when and how the work may be continued under present conditions. All of these were matters of much sincere prayer and consideration during business meetings as well as in our private devotions. Many of such hours come before me now as among the most precious of my entire journey. Whether they were held under the moonlit sky within the sound of the falling waters of the Mahanadi River or in the homes of missionaries or Indian Christians, they carry with them the inspiration and power from above. God seemed so near as we prayed for the wisdom and grace that all of us need in order that the "tangled skein" of circumstances in which we find ourselves caught in this changing time, might be unwound and woven into a pattern that fits into the design set by the Man of Galilee. Having found this may we go forward unitedly and build upon the Word, a living, fruitful church that will accomplish the ends for which it was established. With this we leave the problems in the hands of Him whose servants we are and go forward with the assurance that the outcome cannot be otherwise than according to His will.

XX

SAILING
WITH THE STRATHMORE

The documents that had admitted me to India were in correct form but those that were needed to make possible my leaving gave me trouble. After many trips to the Dhamtari police station I was finally informed that the officer of the District Department at Raipur, some fifty miles away, would have to issue the order. By this time I was nearly ready to leave and there was not sufficient time to negotiate the transaction by mail, hence it was one of the things I had hoped to get accomplished in person while on my way to Bombay. When, however, the auto in which we were traveling refused to function some miles out of the city this plan became impossible. The bus which came along was packed with people even before we attempted to get on but after much shuffling of passengers we finally found room to stand or lean against the seats. We arrived at the station in time to get our luggage and ourselves on the train but not in time to see the District Officer about the exit permits. We then turned this matter over to Arnold Dietzel who was also in the city and left hoping that he would get the proper credentials to us in time for sailing.

I, however, could not leave Raipur without mentioning St. Paul's, the fine Christian school located here, which I visited on an earlier trip. Nor would I pass on without referring to the pleasant hour at the home of Rev. and Mrs. Sybold who entertained us so royally during our brief stay. Institutions such as this one have rendered an immeasurable service to India's young people by helping them to a better way of life as well as to a knowledge that brings them in touch with the "Light of the World" that infuses the soul with the warmth and radiance of the Spirit of God.

Our first stop after leaving Raipur was Nagpur where we were entertained in the home of Judge Bose, who was then Chief Justice of the Supreme Court of the Middle Provinces. His wife, formerly Irene Mott, was in Bombay meeting friends from the United States who came to spend Christmas with her. In India the wife's absence from home does not seem to disrupt the situation as it does in the States. The servants are on duty and household affairs go on in their routine way. Judge Bose comes from a line of lawyers and lives in a spacious and stately house in the midst of an Indian setting with palms and shrubs and flowers. While in the city we called on the Secretary of the Indian Christian Council, the Secretary of the YWCA, and the Superintendent of Public Instruction. During a brief visit at the home of the president of Hyslop College, a Scottish Presbyterian school, we were pleasantly entertained even though the call had not been previously arranged for. These men are all Indian nationals. Most of them are graduates of American universities or seminaries. One could not but be impressed with their deep interest in the affairs of their country. All of them are Christians and manifested a fine attitude toward the work of missions and a deep concern for the cause of Christ.

From Nagpur our route led us via bus line to Warda, the home of the renowned Indian leader, the late Mahatma Gandhi. This rather shaky vehicle was as full of interest as it was of people who were compressed into the meager space which it afforded. It was a remnant of a period that has passed on—outmoded and outdated. Its squeaky, rheumatic joints at first gave me some concern and brought to my mind questions of dependability but its motor, in spite of its wheezy, asthmatic spasms, turned out to be quite reliable and brought us safely to our destination. Clouds arose as we lumbered across the miles to the Ashram of the noted Indian statesman who for years ruled the mind and spirit of the millions who hoped for better things if and when they could get rid of the British and come into control of their country's affairs. This great but humble man set up an establishment outside of Warda which served as an illustration of what can be done without much money by using available materials. The floor and partitions of the house in which he lived were all made of the same material—mud! In the one room was his spinning outfit which he carried with him wherever he went, they say, and when there were a few moments available he occupied himself with making the threads that go into the cloth which makes up the garments of many of the people. The house was set in the midst of trees with a well not far away. From this the water for family use and for irrigation was lifted with a device operated by an ox who trod the path from morning till evening. Other buildings, suitable for meetings of various kinds in which the Mahatma was interested, were located on these same grounds. At the time of our visit a Peace Conference was in progress at which there were delegates from many parts of the world. Among them were men and women of outstanding intelligence and reputation. There were others also, long-haired, bearded, and turbaned men from the western countries with queer costumes and manners. Judging from the conversation of some whom we met en route, they were pacifists, conscientious objectors, war resisters, etc., of every shade and color who gathered here to discuss the problems of the world.

Who is this Mahatma, the great figure that exerted such a tremendous influence upon his people and his country and was for years the leader of India's masses and the center of India's political revolt? By some he was considered a half-naked fakir, a self-deluded visionary, a madman. Others thought of him as a holy man, and the greatest among the great. To the British he was a "thorn in the flesh" but to the Indians he was a hero whose name will, no doubt, be inscribed in the list of the nation's immortals, and perhaps enrolled in the roster of the gods. To many of the western world he is little more than a name.

He was born in 1869 to parents of a respectable family of middle class standing. He was brought up in the strict Hindu tradition. It is said he was not outstanding in the classroom, but he early manifested a deeply sensitive conscience and an ardent love for truth. The first far-reaching decision of his life came at his father's death. At a family conference it was decided that he should go to London to prepare himself for the career of lawyer. His mother, however, objected and was afraid to expose her son to the pressures and temptations of the alien surroundings into which he would be thrown. Before she would give her consent he was required to take an oath to live a celebate life during the period of his study and to touch no meat or wine and live strictly according to the orthodox practices of his mother's religion.

It is said that his life in London was that of a bewildered youngster. He was very sensitive by nature and his ignorance of the customs and practices of his new environment caused him constant embarrassment. He says that he almost starved in the midst of plenty because of his vow not to eat meat. Finally, by accident, he discovered a restaurant for vegetarians and ate his first good meal.

For a time he followed the ways of a sophisticated Englishman. He dressed in the most rakish fashion, took lessons in dancing and elocution, indulged in other extravagances, and ended up in despair. He then settled down to a frugal life and devoted himself diligently to the study of law. During his stay in the world's largest city he secured a Bible from a Christian friend and said that from the very first its message went straight to his heart.

He passed successfully his examinations in 1881 and returned to India. But during his stay in England he had learned more than the law. He had come in contact with Christianity and other philosophies and forces that greatly affected his life. Hence he came home not only a barrister but a man with a new knowledge that kindled in his soul the fires of asceticism, self-renunciation, and service. As a result he was no longer content with the idea of settling down to be merely a practitioner in the field of his chosen profession. He had become a crusader looking for a cause to champion that would be worthy of the ideals he had found. The challenge was not long in coming. In 1893 he accepted a commission to represent a large Indian firm in South Africa. This was the beginning of a legal career that brought him into prominence and furnished him an outlet for the fires that were burning in his bosom. He became the champion of the underprivileged and fought courageously for the removal of the disabilities imposed upon his countrymen by the South African government. Here, too, began his prison career. In the struggle for equality of rights for all races he was jailed four times, mobbed and once left for dead.

During the first World War he loyally supported the British. Following it there were more serious uprisings in his homeland in protest against the Sedition Act whereby persons accused of disloyalty to the state might be deprived of the right to trial by jury. This, together with tax grievances and other legislation and attitudes of the government, called for protests and opposition that resulted in rioting, loss of life, and imprisonment. Again this frail little idealist stepped into the breach. After all other means had failed he finally resorted to fasting while his followers invoked passive resistance as the only available measure which gave promise of success. The results are known to students of history.

Whatever may be said for or against the leadership and teachings of this "holy man," the withdrawal of the British has come about largely through the influence he wielded among his countrymen. He lived to see his dream realized as far as independence is concerned but died by the hand of an assassin while his beloved India was steeped in the blood of fraternal strife. Today his Ashram has become a shrine. Only those whose shoes have been removed dare enter what was once his simple home, to which the feet of many turned in the days of his greatness and power. The place where he once wrought is quiet now except for the voices of those who gather here in the shadows of the past to relearn the lessons the "Sage of Warda" taught. At other times one hears only the footfalls of pilgrims who come from across the world or from the hills and plains, the cities and villages of his homeland, to do homage to their leader and bask in the stillness of the place that was once his home.

We returned to the station in the dusk of the evening to collect our baggage which we had left in charge of a coolie. Within a short time we were on the train en route to Ahmednuggar where Mr. and Mrs. James Smucker now reside. They are working under the American Board (Congregational) which has a mission, a school, and industrial work at this place. It was Christmas Day, nearly noon, when we arrived. We met the usual concourse of people at the station. There were conveyances of all kinds. Most of them, however, belonged to the two-wheeled variety, each one drawn by an antiquated horse or a pair of oxen. It was interesting to see the skill with which the drivers maneuvered their vehicles into position, and then to watch them go down the street with passengers seated with faces backward and legs dangling.

The Smuckers are gracious hosts. The visit with them made us feel that we had come to a bit of homeland. After the Christmas dinner we enjoyed the usual hour of rest in accordance with the custom of the country. Then followed a tea and a short tour of the institutions of the mission. Then we were on our way to Bombay. This turned out to be the dreary end of our journey. With the approach of nightfall we discovered that there were no lights. At the first station-stop we registered our request for repairs. This order was relayed by telegram to the next stop where the matter was duly taken care of. In the meantime we learned that we had no water service in our compartment. With dust sifting in through every crevice water becomes more than a mere luxury, it is a pressing necessity! At each station workmen would appear with tools and fittings that didn't fit until the situation turned from humor to pathos. Our schedule called for a stop of several hours at Pona. Here, after multiplied efforts of trial and failure, much pounding and noise, and enough discussion and planning to get the construction of the whole car under way, the repairs were finally made and we arrived in Bombay on time!

We were again quartered at the Raj Mahal where we had previously stayed. The population, with the exception of Mr. and Mrs. Minnich and the servants, had changed completely. An entirely new set of transients had taken up residence here. Necessary things came first. Fortunately my exit permits had come through. A call at the office of the P & O Steamship Company brought us the information that I was to sail on the Strathmore, a 30,000-ton liner that sails between London and Australia, and that they had reserved a single cabin for me. We arranged to have all our baggage taken to the docks at the proper time for customs inspection and loading. With all these details taken care of, I followed S. M. King from place to place while he was transacting business for the mission. We met people, saw interesting places, and enjoyed greatly the few remaining days of my stay in this large city.

Word reached us that the Catholic Bishop of this area was to arrive on the morning of the day on which I was scheduled to leave. A hurried trip brought us to the pier where the noted prelate was to land, but the crowd that had gathered made it impossible to get close to the scene. From an elevated eminence on top of a stone wall I saw his launch gliding slowly and majestically through the harbor from the dock where he had disembarked to the Arch that is designated the "Gateway to India." Here he stepped on shore amid the plaudits of the multitude that had come to welcome him. A hasty trip to the Raj Mahal for our hand luggage concluded my stay in Bombay.

When we arrived at the dockyard the Strathmore was at the

pier. I went on board ship and was shown the cabin that was to be my home for the next twelve days. The first task was to get my table place and while still in the harbor we had our first meal. Then the gong sounded ordering all visitors ashore. During the next half hour or so while standing at the rails waiting for the crew to lift anchor and move out into the sea a young Indian on the dock was staging an acrobatic show all his own. Coins tossed from the decks by passengers kept him in action till we pulled away from the shore. Then the vessel glided swiftly on and soon Bombay sank beneath the sky line. This last view of India still lingers in my memory—Malabar Hill, the long row of modern apartments along the shore, and India's Gateway! Then I retired for a long rest in my comfortable cabin.

The Strathmore is large and commodious. It was rebuilt since the war and is beautifully finished. Every provision has been made for the comfort and well-being of seafarers and travelers. The swimming pool was well patronized as it always is. The passengers were mostly British or British colonials—people from England, Australia, New Zealand, and India, with a mere sprinkling from the U.S.A. The drinking bar was largely patronized but the crowd was orderly. There was less brazen nudity and all the reckless disregard for what are the accepted rules of propriety in conduct than one finds on American ships.

The crew consisted of British navigators and officers. One met with courteous treatment everywhere—at the table, in the offices, and at the hands of the stewards. All the deck hands were Indians who have served the company long and well. Their fathers, grandfathers, and who knows how far back into the past their forebears, have served before them. They somehow feel that their positions have come to them as a heritage. They do their duty well. On the seas the Captain of a British ship is still master of his domain. The crew is not working for the union, though, no doubt, they all belong to it. They work for the steamship company.

Our first stop was at Aden. Though it was January the weather was hot. Since the stay in this port was short, I did not go ashore. Several passengers came back from their shopping tour with Swiss watches which they purchased at bargain prices. But the timepieces that are on sale here, they say, are those which do not pass the inspection required for the markets in other lands. Even so they were still bargains when compared with what they cost in the countries of the west. As we left Aden I took one last look at the spot where Cain, Adam's erring offspring, is said to repose.

The Red Sea which was so unbearably hot four months before was now pleasant. It was again filled with oil-tankers from England and Europe who carried fuel for the needs of the New World. At Suez we had a twelve-hour wait for the pilot to come and take our convoy through the canal. Salesmen, in their rowboats filled with wares, surrounded us on every side and furnished people a lot of amusement and entertainment as well as an opportunity to spend their money. Sometimes these vendors become a bothersome nuisance, but who would want to miss the noisy, colorful crowd or the bargains they offer?

One day we sailed out of the Red Sea into the choppy waters of the Mediterranean. As the days passed the winds became more chilly and squalls of rain more frequent. One night we sailed past the Rock of Gibraltar. From then on our ship skirted the coast of Spain, Portgugal, and France and one Saturday noon it pulled up at Tilbury, London's dock. The afternoon of arrival at the world's metropolis was gloomy. Skies were overcast, the chilling damps of Britain's winter were upon us.

England was still in the throes of its austerity program. Meat was scarce and at the ordinary eating houses things that passed for sausage and other kinds of ground meat contained little that suggested that it had ever been close to a barnyard or livestock market. Fish, however, was more plentiful. Good food could be obtained at the better restaurants.

216

The seven days of my wait in London became tedious. All along the way I had heard rumors of unheated rooms and days of cold feet and developing chilblains that could have made one panicky had he been so inclined. On my arrival I was surprised to find a room that was rather comfortable as far as the temperature was concerned though no one would have thought of it as being overheated. In this little cubicle I slept at night and stayed in daytime when the weather was too wet or disagreeable to venture outside. Other days I strolled about the city. The busses that carry tourists over the island during the season were laid up for the winter. Other places such as London Tower, museums, and libraries were open. Then there were the streets where the streams of humanity flow. These are always open and constitute places of interest second to none. What a world of people drift hither and yon on the highlanes of this great city! What stories lie hidden within each bosom and what desires and purposes are buried behind the eyes of each passer-by!

One evening I worshiped in what was once a flourishing Baptist congregation. It is now used as a community church. There was an interesting group of some fifty persons present for the meeting. The pulpit from which I spoke is the one that was used by John Bunyan of *Pilgrim's Progress* fame when he was pastor here. One could easily fancy the "shade" of that great soul standing there proclaiming the Word. On another day I in company with John Coffman and his family attended the annual community dinner at a neighborhood hall near the church where people in large numbers came together for fellowship and recreation from what was one time a slum section of the city. The mayor of the suburb clad in his official regalia was present and gave a short address. One evening I attended the weekly dinner which was served by those who worship at this place. I was happy for these contacts and for this fellowship. On the evening before my departure I took dinner at the Coffman home to which a German Mennonite girl now attending a nursing school in a London hospital was also invited. These pleasant hours added greatly to my enjoyment of what might have been days of monotonous gloom in London's fog and chilly winds.

One afternoon the boat-train left the large Victoria Station in London for Southampton where the Queen Mary was loading for New York. The British who depend upon the seaways for much of what they need to live by know how to load ships and how to get passengers through customs and to their assigned places on board with the minimum of time and confusion. Hence with little delay I found myself going up the gangplank and was soon in my cabin, which was shared by a young man from Holland.

Soon after our first meal on board was concluded the vessel left the dock and before I retired we were at one of the ports on the coast of France. The Queen Mary is more than a mere ship —it is a floating city with a population running into the thousands. It has its shops and marts where one can buy all that people who sail the seas desire. In its lounges are libraries stocked with large collections of books to suit the need of every type of reader. But deck games were poorly patronized and the swimming pools were closed. We were sailing on the Atlantic whose moods are unpredictable. The wind was blowing and the ocean was rough. Our table group was all present for the first meal. The next morning when the passengers came on deck and felt the heaving of the ship and saw the whitecaps chase each other wildly across the waters many of them were *"deeply moved"* and betook themselves to the rails where they paid their "tribute" to the sea. Then they took refuge in the solitude of their cabin and what had given promise of a jolly table company was turned into desolation. After a few days some of them came straggling back, shaky and haggard but not very hungry. A few did not make their appearance again until the morning of the day when the ship sailed into New York harbor.

The Queen Mary is a marvel of achievement in the art of

shipbuilding. They say she is designed for speed, long and slender like a greyhound. But she rocks easily which is hard on many people's nerves and plays havoc with their digestion. One who travels certainly wants to make one trip on this Titan of the sea. After that the average person will be just as well satisfied to sail by one of the smaller vessels of lesser renown which do not have as much reputation or speed or group distinction but more fellowship and perhaps greater steadiness against the wind or waves.

We arrived at New York on schedule but were forced to wait outside the harbor for thirty-six hours in a clear shining sun while the city, the docks and piers hung in a dense fog. Finally at three o'clock in the afternoon of the second day anchors were lifted and we were on the way. The Statue of Liberty, symbol of the freedom for which so many are yearning, was in her best mood. As we sailed by there rose in my mind the millions of homeless wanderers—landless, hungry and weary, unloved and unwanted—whom I saw in my travels. Many of them are disowned by their fatherland and some of them are marked for death. They are crowded into countries that are already overflowing. They are looking to America for a home as did your ancestors and mine. Our empty spaces, the spreading plain and unclaimed lands await them and would make them a place to live. Surely among this stranded multitude there are many who would do us good. From such as they the population of our country is made up. Then when I thought of all the legal barriers, the tedious, slow-moving immigration machinery, the traditions, the prejudices, and all the other obstacles that beset their way and bar them from coming, the noble words inscribed on the Statue came back to me empty and filled with mockery:

> Give me your tired, your poor,
> Your huddled masses yearning to breathe free,
> The wretched refuse from your teeming shore,

Send these, the homeless, the tempest-tossed to me:
I lift my lamp beside the golden door.

Maybe someday we will have a new, modern, up-to-date custom house at New York, our eastern metropolis, as they have in
other ports of the world. Until then, we will limp along as best
as we can and appreciate the patience and helpfulness of the
officials whose duty it is to see that bags, trunks, boxes, barrels,
and containers of all kinds are opened for inspection and then
wait with fear and trembling to see what will happen only to
learn how considerate and gracious the officers are when they
have honest people to deal with.

While I was standing by waiting for the Queen Mary to dis-
gorge the contents of her hold and bring my baggage to the surface I was surprised to see my wife and Jane, our little grand-
daughter, coming across the room to where I was. This was a
pleasant and an unexpected meeting. For thirty-six hours they
had waited while the harbor was shrouded in a fog which delayed our entrance. Thoughtful little Jane, upon seeing that I
had no hat, informed me, sympathetically, that they had brought
me one. In accordance with a long-standing habit of forgetting
things, I had left mine in India—the trail of my lost hats now
reaches around the world! Baggage transfers delayed our leaving the city for another day, much to Jane's delight. This enabled her to see more of the tall buildings and eat several more
meals at Tony's. Then followed a night's ride on the comfortable "Commodore Vanderbilt" and I was once more at home,
the most cherished spot on earth! All day the words of John
Howard Payne rang in my ears as I wandered among the
birches, the elms, maples, and shrubs that I had left some six
months earlier:

'Mid pleasures and palaces though we may roam,
Be it ever so humble, there's no place like home;
A charm from the skies seems to hallow us there,
Which, seek through the world, is ne'er met with elsewhere.

An exile from home, splendor dazzles in vain;
O give me my lowly thatched cottage again!
The birds singing gaily that came at my call,
Give me them—and the peace of mind—dearer than all!